Passing through a Gate

Also by John Balaban

POETRY

Empires (Copper Canyon Press, 2019)

Like Family (Red Dragonfly, 2009)

Path, Crooked Path (Copper Canyon Press, 2006)

Locusts at the Edge of Summer: New & Selected Poems
    (Copper Canyon Press, 1997, 2003)

Words for My Daughter (Copper Canyon Press, 1991)

Blue Mountain (Unicorn Press, 1982)

After Our War (University of Pittsburgh Press, 1974)

TRANSLATION

Ca Dao Việt Nam: Vietnamese Folk Poetry (Copper Canyon Press, 2003)

Spring Essence: The Poetry of Hồ Xuân Hương (Copper Canyon Press, 2000)

Vietnam: A Traveler's Literary Companion, with Nguyen Qui Duc
    (Whereabouts Press, 1996)

NONFICTION

Remembering Heaven's Face: A Story of Rescue in Wartime Vietnam
    (University of Georgia Press, 2002)

Vietnam: The Land We Never Knew, photography by Geoffrey Clifford
    (Chronicle Books, 1989)

FICTION

Coming Down Again (Simon & Schuster/Fireside, 1989)

The Hawk's Tale (Harcourt Brace Jovanovich, 1988)

Passing through a Gate:

POEMS, ESSAYS, AND TRANSLATIONS

John Balaban

COPPER CANYON PRESS

PORT TOWNSEND, WASHINGTON

Cover art: Courtesy of Ian Campbell

Copper Canyon Press is in residence at Fort Worden State Park in Port Townsend, Washington, under the auspices of Centrum. Centrum is a gathering place for artists and creative thinkers from around the world, students of all ages and backgrounds, and audiences seeking extraordinary cultural enrichment.

LIBRARY OF CONGRESS CATALOGING-IN-PUBLICATION DATA
Names: Balaban, John, 1943– author.
Title: Passing through a gate : poems, essays, and translations / John
   Balaban.
Other titles: Passing through a gate (Compilation)
Description: Port Townsend, Washington : Copper Canyon Press, 2024. |
   Summary: "A collection of poetry and prose by John Balaban"— Provided
   by publisher.
Identifiers: LCCN 2023039092 (print) | LCCN 2023039093 (ebook) |
   ISBN 9781556596919 (paperback) | ISBN 9781619322905 (epub)
Subjects: LCGFT: Poetry. | Essays.
Classification: LCC PS3552.A44 P37 2024 (print) | LCC PS3552.A44 (ebook) |
   DDC 811/.54—dc23/eng/20231020
LC record available at https://lccn.loc.gov/2023039092
LC ebook record available at https://lccn.loc.gov/2023039093

9 8 7 6 5 4 3 2 FIRST PRINTING

COPPER CANYON PRESS
Post Office Box 271
Port Townsend, Washington 98368
www.coppercanyonpress.org

for Lonnie, as ever,
and our daughter, Tally

CONTENTS

Enduring Worth

Across a body of work that spans fifty years, fourteen books, and four genres, John Balaban has carried on a passionate conversation with history and its figures—some unnamed and some renowned. In novels, essays, memoirs, poems, and translations, he celebrates literary legacies while challenging the legacy of empire and its many modes of violence. Balaban and his contemporaries, in their work and through their mentorship, have set an example for politically and ethically engaged writing. Their influence can be seen across the landscape of contemporary literature. As much as this retrospective collection represents the work of one writer, it also serves to document Balaban's commitment to an expanding community of poets, writers, teachers, and activists.

From his earliest poems in *After Our War* (1974), a finalist for the National Book Award, and his *Words for My Daughter* (1991), winner of the National Poetry Series, through to his outstanding memoir, *Remembering Heaven's Face* (2002), and his most recent poems in *Empires* (2019), John Balaban has moved intently between the domain of the personal and the communal. In his early works, Balaban offers personal perspectives to shine light on subjects transcending the self, as in those essays that begin in his experience in Vietnam with the International Voluntary Services during the American War and that end in his translations of Vietnamese folk songs. In his early poems we also read about the poverty and alienation of his childhood. When I worked with John on *Path, Crooked Path* (2006), he would tell me how his life had been significantly marked by violence, how he had eventually left home for mentors who introduced him to literature and the arts. Balaban's later poems similarly leave the familiar to wander the contested lands of the American West—in search of what his nation signifies—or to explore the haunted eastern European landscape of his ancestors. Wherever his poems have ventured, they have recounted friendships, pursued memories, and documented close calls, heroic moments, and ceaseless instances of quiet dignity and self-examination.

The epigraph at the start of his collection *Locusts at the Edge of Summer* (1997, 2003) quotes Dante's *De vulgari eloquentia*: "The proper subjects for poetry are love, virtue, and war." Throughout this book, one reads of love and virtue. The poems highlight friendships and chance encounters and recall allegiances to other writers and traditions, enacting Balaban's unwavering belief in the *word* and its power to transform across history, carried by the voices of many others. With such an appreciation for shared tradition and intellectual kinship, Balaban's writing is free of self-important frippery and pretension, even as he valorizes the heroic and celebrates the dignity and integrity of those who resist subjugation—be it political or poetic. Given his dedication to the pursuit of justice, Balaban occasionally displays consternation and rage at forces that seek to undermine individual ambition or that demand an individual follow a plan of action unquestioningly. In his writing, there is a rebellious, sometimes pugnacious, defense of the quotidian. Balaban champions the unseen and overlooked, maintains enduring faith in and respect for the downtrodden individual as well as the disenfranchised populace. In this way, he joins the long and noble tradition of the writer as advocate for marginalized peoples and literatures.

I first discovered Balaban's *After Our War* as an undergraduate, and I read him in conversation with Yusef Komunyakaa, Tim O'Brien, Michael Herr, and others who were writing about the American War in Vietnam. They helped me see the role of literature in shaping my perspective of politics and history. Later, when I was still new to a career in publishing, I discovered *Words for My Daughter*. That book has been part of my life for over three decades now, and the title poem never fails to bring tears to my eyes. John's writing sustains me as a reader; his writing encourages me, too, as an editor who values the connections and communities established on a page, in a book, across a body of work. Shortly after discovering *Words for My Daughter*, I started working as John's editor, learning from him and witnessing his passion for poetry, his unwavering commitment to forwarding poetic tradition. To paraphrase Walter Benjamin, writing is a deeply engaged form of reading, and in Balaban's poems I have found a passionate reader who is writing traditions forward. His work is concerned with the human project far beyond the self.

I've had the great fortune of working with John Balaban now for thirty years, and have shared many personally and professionally formative moments with him. Throughout that time he has repeatedly advocated not only for publishers, but for an entire community of poets—including younger poets such as Tyree Daye, Natalie Diaz, Agha Shahid Ali, Paul Perry, and the Barbadian Poet Laureate Esther Philips; colleague-mentors such as W.S. Merwin and Denise Levertov; and long-dead poets whose work had never previously been translated. Early on in our friendship, John told me about his adventures collecting and translating *ca dao*—folk songs—in wartime Vietnam. Here, he was asking ordinary farmers and merchants to sing him a favorite poem. In the wake of that work, he told me of his desire to bring the poetry of Hồ Xuân Hương to Western audiences, explaining to me how important she was. He was not content to simply translate her poetry. Instead he wanted to collaborate with Vietnamese scholars and typesetters to highlight the lost writing system in which she wrote—and in which Vietnamese culture, history, and teachings were propagated across two millennia. This was not just a book; it was a mission to use his passion for literature and skills as a translator for a larger project that has reach beyond the literary world. Balaban's persistent curiosity has been a hallmark of his groundbreaking work as a translator, and he has used some of his privilege as a citizen of the richest country on earth to "return" to Vietnam some of the richness lost to it because of countries like his own.

Early in his writing life, in his years as a student interested in translating literature and his time spent with activist-writers such as Levertov and Merwin, Balaban invited others' expertise and influence into his own writing. He noted in the essay "Poetcraft," published in *The Writer's Chronicle,* that "the poet of enduring worth is both maker and prophet." In that same essay Balaban quotes Ralph Waldo Emerson as saying "every word was once a poem," before Balaban himself explains that "every word is also a rhythm, or at minimum a single stress about to join with another syllable into possible rhythm, [and] it is the rhythm of words that heightens our emotions in a poem." I'd add that every poet is at minimum a single voice that joins in the chorus of history and the legacy of shared and remade voices, and over the course of nearly sixty years, Balaban has worthily refined his own voice in order to join the community of literature. Each time he recounts a moment of personal history, each time he celebrates the work of a student or mentor, each time he advocates for the marginalized and their stories, searches for the poem within every word, he adds one more syllable to the greater rhythm of literature.

Balaban writes in "Poetcraft" that poets' shaping and making are "built into the very word that we are known by"; his integrity and dedication are likewise built into each poem by which he is known. Balaban's poems are carefully imagined events that call on the greatness within the seemingly doomed human experiment. Over his distinguished career, Balaban has worked to make and remake himself as a writer and translator. His approach to craft and his commitment as a literary citizen form a model for how we as writers and readers might position ourselves in the literary landscape. *Passing through a Gate* invites us to join in the chorus, to sustain the love, virtue, and belief carried in every word. You will, I trust, find poems to return to time and again, as if seeking the company of a good friend.

Michael Wiegers

Passing through a Gate

Walking Down into Cebolla Canyon

Then, truly unhappy, terrified by Fate, wearied by the empty sky,
Dido prayed for death.

VIRGIL, *THE AENEID* 4.450–451

1

Everything about us, for better or worse,

we make ourselves, with marvelous exceptions:

The snow peaks rinsed in rose light

at dusk on the Sangre de Cristo range.

The bleached, broken jaw of a mule deer

its teeth scattered among cactus wreaths

beside the trail, down from the mesa

where the river stammers against volcanic

rocks and pools, where spooked trout skim

through aspen leaves tumbling in clear water.

2

This river cut through centuries of rock

to our time when all assertions are suspect,

to our century of assurances gone mute,

where we, deserted like Dido before her pyre

or Raleigh pacing The Lie in the Tower,

look up to see "a wearying, empty sky"

and gag on words like sour meats

stewed in the stomach of a haggis sheep.

So, pity the poets, whose work is words,

reduced to blather or fiery silences

as the gods who breathed the Word expire.

3

This vast rubble offers its one blessing:

everything it says is true—parched mesa,

willow water, fox skull, circling raven,

tarantula, deer turd, singing wren.

One wanders down past living metaphors.

Where life is threatened, few lies are told.

Under a blank sky one clambers down

collapsed ledges clustered with paintbrush.

Small. Alone. No better than a bug.

4

Accepting these terms, one takes a place

offered all along by the ribboned stream

calling up from the bouldered canyon floor,

to stand here at dusk and stare at spilling water

near a wren jigging on a jagged slab

as the river leaps by through lunar wastes

where trout, coyote, magpie, cougar, prosper

in the innocence which humans find in love

bringing us the water's benediction:

"The streams we play in flow sweet water.
Anyone might drink here and be refreshed.
All day, sunlight strikes the river clear,
At dusk, the current ripples with a moon.
Love like water makes the canyons bloom."

Forsan et haec olim meminisse juvabit.
VIRGIL, *THE AENEID* 1.203

Someday, perhaps, it will help to remember these things.
(AENEAS, TO HIS CREW OF SURVIVORS,
AFTER THE TROJAN WAR)

War Poetry, Political Poetry, and the Invisible Powers

The problem for a poet in writing about modern war is that, while he can only deal with events of which he has first-hand knowledge—invention, however imaginative, is bound to be fake—his poems must somehow transcend mere journalistic reportage. In a work of art, the single event must be seen as an element in a universally significant pattern: the area of the pattern actually illuminated by the artist's vision is always more or less limited, but one is aware of its extending beyond what we see far into time and space.

W.H. AUDEN, PREFACE TO THE FIRST EDITION OF
LINCOLN KIRSTEIN'S *RHYMES OF A PFC*

One day in Hanoi, where our Nôm foundation was working at the National Library to digitize its several thousand ancient texts, I took the day off to visit the ancient Temple of Literature, founded in 1076 after the Vietnamese had finally driven out their Chinese overlords. Until 1919, when the temple's function ended under the French, this was the academy where Vietnam trained its governing elite in poetry, history, and philosophy, selecting gifted students from all social classes in the belief that a mind trained and tested in such subjects is a quick, sharp, and careful mind, and that such minds are important resources to the nation.

One enters the temple grounds through a large stone gate topped with recoiling dragons, indicating royal rule and its mandate from heaven. One then proceeds past gardens and ponds through another large gateway under a tile-roofed balcony where, over the centuries, new graduates once declaimed their poetry. Perhaps the most striking thing one then sees is rows of six-foot stone blocks standing on the backs of massive stone turtles. On these blocks are carved the names of those who graduated from the temple and entered Vietnam's civil service. Even today, hundreds of years after these graduates served the nation, one can see their descendants lighting incense sticks and placing them before those stone blocks in familial veneration.

Farther on, in a room inside the temple itself, is a square stone carved in Chinese characters, and next to it translations into modern Vietnamese and English:

Virtuous and talented men are state-sustaining elements. The strength and prosperity of a state depend on it[s] stable vitality and it becomes weaker as such vitality fails. That is why all the saint emperors and clear-sighted kings didn't fail in seeing to the formation of men of talent and the employment of literati to develop this vitality. (Examination Stele, Đại Bảo Dynasty, Third Year [1442])

Literati? Literary people as "state-sustaining elements"? How on earth, we Americans might ask, can citizens trained in literary skills be "state-sustaining elements"? Why would the Vietnamese royal court set up a university for its best and brightest, regardless of class or wealth, and then train them largely in poetry, history, and philosophy?

If that seems a little far-fetched, consider this: Confucius, the Chinese philosopher to whom the Vietnamese Temple of Literature is dedicated, along with the Duke of Chou (this after the Chinese were finally driven out), was once asked the perennial philosophical question of fourth-century China—as it was the perennial question for Socrates in Plato's *Republic*—"What would you first do if allowed to rule a kingdom?" Confucius's reply, as recorded in his *Analects*, was "to correct language." Here is the exchange from book 8 of the *Analects*, written around 400 BCE. The useful application of the Confucian reply to our affairs today is obvious:

Tzu-lu said, "If the prince of Wei were waiting for you to come and administer his country for him, what would be your first measure?"

The Master said, "It would certainly be to correct language."

Tzu-lu said, "Did I hear you right? Surely what you say has nothing to do with the matter. Why should language be corrected?"

The Master said, "Lu! How simple you are! A gentleman, when things he does not understand are mentioned, should maintain an attitude of reserve. If language is incorrect, then what is said does not concord with what was meant; and if what is said does not concord with what was meant, what is to be done cannot be effected. If what is to be done cannot be effected, then society falls apart."

Such precision in the use of words is, of course, a lifelong pleasure in and of itself, but it has immense practical value as well. Without such precision in the way we communicate with ourselves, with one another as a society, and with the world beyond, our private and public affairs falter and fall apart. Precision in the use of words is the talent that lends all other professions and skills their usefulness. It is a skill that goes beyond utilitarian technology. Such precision in speech, writing, and the reading of complex works of the human imagination brings to its practitioners and to their societies a more enriched sense of self and an inevitable moral expansion.

This skill, most notably found in poetry, is indeed "a state-sustaining" endeavor. It is no mere curiosity that from Vietnam's earliest nationhood its rulers and foreign emissaries were always known poets. The eighteenth-century ambassador to China, Nguyễn Du, decorated by his emperor as a "pillar of the nation," is also Vietnam's most famous poet. In modern times, Hồ Chí Minh wrote quite good poetry in Vietnamese and in Chinese. The North Vietnamese head of delegation to the 1973 Paris Peace Accords was Xuân Thủy, known first as a poet.

Traditionally, the chief poetic vehicle for study and composition was the "regulated" *lǜshī* verse form made classic by the Chinese master Tu Fu in the eighth century and called *tho đường luật* in Vietnamese. It is always eight lines, seven syllables to a line, rhyming usually on the first, second, fourth, sixth, and eighth lines, and requiring syntactic parallel structure in the middle four. For several East Asian societies it became the main lyric vehicle for centuries, serving them in the way the sonnet served the West. This form—whether written in Vietnamese or in Chinese—streamed with history and culture in generations of individuals possessing "bright mind." As the stone tablet at the Temple of Literature suggests, the strength and prosperity of a state depend on its stable vitality created by men and women who are trained to inquire, sharpen their minds, and expand their souls by an active engagement, as we would say, with "the best words in the best order," which is how Coleridge defined poetry, as recorded in *Table Talk* (1835).

This notion of poetry's affecting voice resulting in moral action is increasingly foreign to us. The idea that a poem can change political events probably seems quaint, if not preposterous. Yet even today Vietnamese will gamble on a person's ability to aptly end a poem, and political debates can be won by an appropriate poetic quotation. Indeed, legend has it that a Chinese invasion was once turned back by the following poem, supposedly painted with honey on banana leaves that were eaten by ants, the result causing panic in the invading troops. Whether this really happened isn't as significant as the legend itself and its existence in popular belief:

南 國 山 河 南 帝 居	Our mountains and rivers belong to the Southern Ruler.
截 然 定 分 在 天 書	This is written in the Celestial Book.
如 何 逆 虜 來 侵 犯	Those who try to conquer this land
汝 等 行 看 取 敗 虛	Will surely suffer defeat. (Marshall Lý Thường Kiệt, 1019–1105)

One is reminded of poetry's effect on more recent human events by George Washington's decision on December 26, 1776, the eve of his attack on Trenton. As his flotilla of farmers prepared to cross the Delaware, in the night, in a blizzard, he had his troops assemble to hear a reading of Thomas Paine's just-published poetic essay regarding "summer soldiers and sunshine patriots." Their subsequent attack, and perhaps that reading, changed the course of the war.

Christmas Eve at Washington's Crossing

Out on the freezing Delaware, ice sheets bob the surface, breaking
against granite pilings of the colonial river inn swept by winter storm.

Gusts of snow blow off a sandbar and sink in plunging currents
where a line of ducks paddles hard against the blizzard

as cornfields on the Jersey banks are whisked into bits
of stalks and broken sheaves spinning in the squalls.

This is where, one such Christmas night, the tall courtly general with
   bad teeth
risked his neck and his rebels to cross the storming river and rout the
   Hessians.

⸺ ⸺

What made them think they could succeed? ... farmers mostly,
leaving homesteads to load cannon into Durham boats

to row into the snowstorm, then march all night to Trenton,
saving the Republic for Valley Forge and victory at Yorktown.

Before crossing, legend says, they assembled in the snow to hear
Paine's new essay about summer soldiers and sunshine patriots.

What words could call us all together now? On what riverbank?
For what common good would we abandon all?

But what about the success of political poetry today, including, say,
the Joseph Biden inaugural poem written by Amanda Gorman? Why
do some poems stay alive in us while others never even take hold? Some
poems disappear as their immediate events fade from memory. But why
do others endure? And why do a handful of poems referring to politics or
war take hold when most are immediately forgotten? Do poems based in
the shocks of warfare or in popular political sentiment belong to a differ-
ent category of aesthetics?

In a letter to me in Vietnam in 1968, in response to some poems I had
mailed him, my former teacher John Barth wrote:

The poems get it said, even to me, who do not find very much war
poetry successful if it has more than one topical proper name in it.
Most of Lowell's and Bly's & Who-Have-You's Vietnam verse, sin-
cere as its horrification and indignation is, will fare as badly as Karl
Shapiro's V-Letter poems, I believe, once the bloody war is over
and the verses have to survive on their excellence alone.

Nonetheless, Randall Jarrell, writing in his *Fifty Years of American Poetry,* says this about Shapiro's style in his war poems: "Karl Shapiro's poems are fresh and young and rash and live; their hard clear outlines, their flat bold colors create a world like that of a knowing and skillful neo-primitive painting, without any of the confusion or profundity of atmosphere, or aerial perspective, but with notable visual and satiric force." "Neoprimitive," "without any of the confusion or profundity of atmosphere." Not much in the way of praise.

During World War II, Shapiro was stationed as a military clerk in Australia and New Guinea. (Perhaps a poet's proximity or distance from the battlefield is one factor in a war poem's success, even for accomplished, established poets like Robert Lowell.) Indeed, in the 2014 edition of his centuries-spanning collection, the *New Oxford Book of War Poetry,* Jon Stallworthy writes:

> "The charge against a poem like Lowell's 'Women, Children, Babies, Cows, Cats' is that, far from shocking an exposed nerve, it has the numbing effect of second-hand journalism," adding with regard to Vietnam, that "a problem for many American poets then aspiring to be war poets was that, rightly perceiving it to be an unjust war, they could not participate as servicemen or women; and lacking first-hand experience, could not write convincingly of the war 'on the ground.'"

Yet this does not explain the many forgettable poems in the 1985 anthology (in which I am included) called *Carrying the Darkness,*[1] edited by a foremost poet of that war and including no less than seventy-five poets, all witnesses to the war, writing mostly in loose free verse, offering raw scenes and harsh ironies in often conversational, colloquial, cool, and hip dictions. The anthology included for its readers back home not only topical names but also a three-page glossary of military terms, slang, and war-related abbreviations: AK-47, ao dai, ARVN, beaucoup, beaucoup dien cai dau, berm, BOQ/PX, etc., ending with Zippo, zoomie.

Other factors must be working to ensure a war poem's success besides having the author's feet on the battlefield. The connection of a poem with its readers surely must have to do not only with its topic—war or whatever—*but with essentials of craft,* the poet's ability to summon appropriate use of imagery, rhythm, sound play, and argument. As Ezra Pound put it in his 1934 *ABC of Reading,* "you still charge words with meaning mainly in three ways, called phanopoeia, melopoeia, logopoeia. You use a word to throw a visual image on to the reader's imagination, or you charge it by sound, or you use groups of words to do this."[2]

In the blither of twenty-first-century media that floods our eyes and ears each day, it is no wonder if poetry seems weak and irrelevant. In *Humboldt's Gift,* Saul Bellows's powerful novel based on his brilliant and crazed poet friend, the catastrophic Delmore Schwartz, Bellow describes poets as "poor loonies" and seems to cast a cold view on the importance of poets in modern society:

> The country is proud of its dead poets. It takes terrific satisfaction in the poets' testimony that the USA is too tough, too big, too much, too rugged, that American reality is overpowering. And to be a poet is a school thing, a skirt thing, a church thing. The weakness of the spiritual powers is proved in the childishness, madness, drunkenness, and despair of these martyrs. Orpheus moved stones and trees. But a poet can't perform a hysterectomy or send a vehicle out of the solar system. Miracle and power no longer belong to him. So poets are loved, but loved because they just can't make it here. They exist to light up the enormity of the awful tangle and justify the cynicism of those who say, "If *I* were not such a corrupt, unfeeling bastard, creep, thief, and vulture, I couldn't get through this either. . . ."[3]

That is to say, their poetic artistry of words means very little compared to the *real* skills, the *visible, demonstrable* powers of technology.

In modern America, even poets will seem to claim that "poetry makes nothing happen," as in W.H. Auden's famous passage in his "In Memory of W.B. Yeats":

For poetry makes nothing happen: it survives
In the valley of its making where executives
Would never want to tamper, flows on south
From ranches of isolation and the busy griefs,
Raw towns that we believe and die in; it survives,
A way of happening, a mouth.

Poetry survives. It is a way of happening. A mouth.

Auden's apparent criticism in fact points to poetry's power, including that of war poetry and political poetry. When its voice is memorable, poetry's "mouth" can speak to our innermost selves and to the universe beyond us. This is no slight thing. *This changes everything.* With this qualification, poetry becomes as essential for us now as it ever was—even if it is hardly read today and rarely reviewed—for if (and when) poetry gives us a "mouth," a voice to express our most private and public concerns, poetry makes *everything* happen, extending our own voice and human self, opening paths to address our inmost thoughts and the universe outside of us. Poetry "objectifies the subjective; subjectifies the objective," as the philosopher Susanne Langer argues in her essay on the cultural importance of art.[4]

But how does any art form make things happen? By changing us.

And how does it change us? By opening in us a new sense of ourselves in the world.

My "if (and when)" above refers to both the skills of craft employed and the "genius" of the poet evoking those skills as needed for the task at hand. Early in our English speculations about the uses of poetry, Sir Philip Sidney wrote in his *Defence of Poesy* (1580) that "a poet no industry can make if his own genius be not carried into it."

The philosopher therefore and the historian are they which would win the goal, the one by precept, the other by example; but both not having both, do both halt. . . .

Now doth the peerless poet perform both; for whatsoever the philosopher says should be done, he gives a perfect picture of it in some one by whom he presupposes it was done, so as he couples the general notion with the particular example. A perfect picture, I say; for he yields to the powers of the mind an image of that whereof the philosopher bestows but a wordish description, which doth neither strike, pierce, nor possess the sight of the soul so much as that other doth.

Genius and craft. The first is impossible to talk about and the second can't be talked about enough, especially when engaging young writers. As with any poetry, mere rhetorical claim or assertion may be the start of a poem but rarely are they its completion. Rhetorically determined poetry isn't less or different or necessarily off-putting because of its topic but for its want of persuasive skills.

Some years ago Mona Van Duyn, then the poet laureate of the United States, was interviewed by Ted Koppel on his ABC television show *Nightline.* Mr. Koppel must have ticked off Ms. Van Duyn because here is her exchange:

Mr. Koppel, I have watched you over the years as you challenge, manipulate, contradict, humiliate the world's leaders, the world's visible powers. Those powers are very great; they can change the world. Now you are in a new world, the world of invisible powers, the world of literature, of poem and story. These do not force their powers upon their subjects, who freely choose to submit to them. You cannot contradict, challenge, manipulate, or humiliate them. They work invisibly—they widen and deepen the human imagination; they increase empathy (without which no being is truly human); they train the emotions to employ themselves with more appropriateness and precision; they change or modify the very language in which human thought is formed. Like love, but stronger, since love's power is limited by mortality, they are holders and keepers of what Time would otherwise take away from us—the world, both natural (its creatures, colors, shapes, textures, sounds, smells, tastes) and the social (the others we love or hate or have never known, their voices, appearances, assumptions, the inner and outer contexts of their lives). These powers, too, are very great; *they can change the self.*[5]

NOTES

1. *Carrying the Darkness,* W.D. Ehrhart, ed. (Avon Books, 1985).
2. Ezra Pound, *ABC of Reading* (Faber and Faber, 1934), p. 37.
3. Saul Bellow, *Humboldt's Gift* (Viking Press, 1975), p. 118. Note also: "Pox take your orators and poets, they spoile lives and histories." —John Aubrey, letter to Anthony Wood, in *Two Antiquaries: A Selection from the Correspondence of John Aubrey and Anthony Wood,* edited by Maurice Balme (Durham Academic Press, 2001), p. 91.
4. Susanne K. Langer, "The Cultural Importance of the Arts," *Journal of Aesthetic Education* 1, no. 1 (Spring 1966), p. 12.
5. Mona Van Duyn, "Matters of Poetry," a lecture delivered at the Library of Congress, 1993.

Along the Mekong

1. CROSSING ON THE MEKONG FERRY, READING
THE AUGUST 14 *NEW YORKER*

Near mud-tide mangrove swamps, under the drilling sun,
the glossy cover, styled green print, struck the eye:
trumpet-burst yellow blossoms, grapevine leaves
—nasturtiums or pumpkin flowers? They twined
in tangles by our cottage in Pennsylvania.
Inside, another article by Thomas Whiteside.
2, 4, 5-T, teratogenicity in births;
South Vietnam 1/7 defoliated; residue
in rivers, foods, and mothers' milk.
With a scientific turn of mind I can understand
that malformations in lab mice may not occur in children
but when, last week, I ushered harelipped, tusk-toothed kids
to surgery in Saigon, I wondered, what did they drink
that I have drunk? What dioxin, picloram, arsenic
have knitted in my cells, in my wife now carrying
our first child. Pigs were squealing in a truck.
Through the slats, I saw one lather the foam in its mouth.

2. RIVER MARKET

Under the tattered umbrellas, piles of live eels
sliding in flat tin pans. Catfish flip for air.
Sunfish, gutted and gilled, cheek plates snipped.
Baskets of ginger roots, ginseng, and garlic cloves;
pails of shallots, chives, green citrons. Rice grain
in pyramids. Pig halves knotted with mushy fat.
Beef haunches hung from fist-size hooks. Sorcerers,
palmists, and, under a tarp: thick incense, candles.

Why, a reporter, or a cook, could write this poem
if he had learned dictation. But what if I said,
simply suggested, that all this blood fleck,
muscle rot, earth root and earth leaf, scraps
of glittery scales, fine white grains, fast talk,
gut grime, crab claws, bright light, sweetest smells
—Said: a human self: a mirror held up before.

3. WAITING FOR A BOAT TO CROSS BACK

Slouched on a bench under some shade,
I overhear that two men shot each other on the street,
and I watch turkey cocks drag cornstalk fans
like mad, rivaling kings in kabuki
sweeping huge sleeve and brocaded train.
The drab hens huddle, beak to beak,
in queenly boredom of rhetoric and murder.
A mottled cur with a greasepaint grin
laps up fish scales and red, saw-toothed gills
gutted from panfish at the river's edge.

The Guard at the Binh Thuy Bridge

How still he stands as mists begin to move,
as curling, morning billows creep across

his cooplike, concrete sentry perched mid-bridge
over mid-muddy river. Stares at bush-green banks

which bristle rifles, mortars, men—perhaps.
No convoys shake the timbers. No sound

but water slapping boat sides, bank sides, pilings.
He's slung his carbine barrel down to keep

the boring dry, and two banana-clips instead of one
are taped to make, now, forty rounds instead

of twenty. Droplets bead from stock to sight;
they bulb, then strike his boot. He scrapes his heel,

and sees no box bombs floating toward his bridge.
Anchored in red morning mist a narrow junk

rocks its weight. A woman kneels on deck
staring at lapping water. Wets her face.

Idly the thick Rach Binh Thuy slides by.
He aims. At her. Then drops his aim. Idly.

Mau Than

a poem at Tet for To Lai Chanh

1

Friend, the Old Man that was last year
has had his teeth kicked in; in tears
he spat back blood and bone, and died.
Pielike, the moon has carved the skies
a year's worth to the eve. It is Tet
as I sit musing at your doorstep,
as the yellowed leaves scratch and clutter.
The garden you dug and plotted
before they drafted you, is now
stony, dry, and wanting a trowel.
"For my wife," you said, taking a plum,
but the day never came nor will it come
to bring your bride from Saigon.
Still the boats fetch stone, painted eyes on
their prows, plowing the banana-green river;
and neighbor children splash and shiver
where junks wait to unload their rock.
But shutters locked, the door of your house is locked.

2

A year it was of barbarities
each heaped on the other like stones
on a man stoned to death.
One counts the ears on the GI's belt.
Market meats come wrapped in wrappers
displaying Viet Cong disemboweled.
Cries come scattering like shot.
You heard them and I heard them.

The night you left I turned off Hoa Binh
and saw a mined jeep, the charred family.
A Vietnamese cop minded the wreckage:
his gold buckteeth were shining
in a smile like a bright brass whistle.
Can you tell me how the Americans,
officers and men, on the night of
the mortaring, in the retching hospital,
could snap flash photos of the girl whose
vagina was gouged out by mortar fragments?
One day we followed in a cortege
of mourners, among the mourners, slowing walking,
hearing the clop of the monk's knocking stick.

3

If there were peace, this river would be
a peaceful place. Here at your door
thoughts arrive like rainwater, dotting,
overspreading a dry, porous rock.
In a feathery drizzle, a man and wife
are fishing the river. The sidling waves
slap at her oar as she ladles the water
and fixes the boat with bored precision.
His taut wrists fling whirring weights;
the flying net swallows a circle of fish.
His ear wears a raindrop like a jewel.
Here at evening one might be as quiet
as the rain blowing faintly off
the eaves of a rice boat sliding home.
Coming to this evening
after a rain, I found a buff bird
perched in the silvery-green branches
of a water-shedding spruce. It was
perched like a peaceful thought. Then

I thought of the Book of Luke and, indeed,
of the nobleman who began a sojourn
to find a kingdom and return.

4

Out of the night, wounded
with the gibberings of dogs,
wheezing with the squeaks of rats,
out of the night, its belly split
by jet whine and mortar blast,
scissored by the claws of children,
street sleepers, ripping their way free
from cocoons of mosquito netting
to flee the rupturing bursts
and the air dancing with razors
—out, I came, to safe haven.
Nor looked, nor asked further.
Who would? What more? I said.
I said: Feed and bathe me.
In Japan I climbed Mt. Hiei in midwinter.
The deer snuffled my mittens.
The monkeys came to beg.
I met Moses meeting God in the clouds.
The cold wind cleared my soul.
The mountain was hidden in mist. Friend,
I am back to gather the blood in a cup.

The Gardenia in the Moon

for David Lane Gitelson, 1942–1968

1. BACK HOME IN PENNSYLVANIA WOODS

The wind was husking, hushing, hosting,
worrying the slimed leaves of the wood.
Moon's light, thick as witches' butter,
stuck to branch bark and to lifting leaves.
Standing under fitful oaks, under Orion
bullying the gods, I saw car lights
stabbing past the rainblacked trunks,
and heard peacocks shriek, an owl
hoot. Men had landed on the moon.
As men shot dirty films in dirty motel rooms,
guerrillas sucked cold rice and fish.
Windspooked leaves scratched my cheek.
Blood on the bark stung my hand.
In a puddle's moon eye I saw a shape:
A machine gun was cracking like slapping sticks.
A yelling man smacked into the smooth canal.

2. I.V.S. MEMORANDUM

TO: Dan Whitfield   DATE: Jan. 30, 1968

FROM: Roger Montgomery

SUBJECT: A Chronology

On Friday evening, Jan. 26, I met the plane coming in from Long Xuyên,
bringing Tom Fox, who was to change planes and go on to Saigon, after
visiting Phil Yang in Long Xuyên. Tom brought the first word that Dave
had been captured and reported killed. After hearing all of the informa-
tion that Tom had, I quickly returned to the CORDS office to call you

and relay the small amount of info that we had. That evening I called Col. Lane in Long Xuyên, and also Bob Flores called me in Cần Thỏ. The first reports were that a man who had been called a "taxi driver" (perhaps of a water taxi boat?) had reported to officials in Huế Đuc district that he had seen Dave captured by four VC and taken off a distance into a woodsy section and then heard four shots. That evening there was also a report that somebody in Huế Đuc had seen a body. It was not confirmed by any American or Vietnamese Government official that it was Dave and there was no certainty where it was. The next morning I drove to Long Xuyên with John Balaban. . . .

Col. Lane, who in his briefing to John and me expressed his dislike for Dave and related how they had had serious disagreements (especially concerning the bombing incident reported in Dave's last monthly report), said that they were making all efforts to recover his body but that he had been consulting his rule books all morning to find out if the military should handle civilians' bodies, and couldn't find a guiding ruling. . . .

. . . [Dave] also was onto something that was extremely sensitive, which he had mentioned to Tom Fox and me just the previous Wednesday (or Thursday) that one day prior to Senator Edward Kennedy's trip to Huế Đuc district to visit the refugees that the refugee chief had come out and told the refugees that if they spoke out complaining to Senator Kennedy about treatment in the refugee camp that he would have them killed or imprisoned or such.

3. FLYING HIS BODY HOME

Think of hot mercury trickling out
or molten silver pouring in a dish.
The webs and sluggish river loops
winked up the sun's burst blooms
as the plane droned home to Saigon.
Zipped in a green vinyl sack
shutting the stinks together, the body
shook on the rivet-rattling floor.
Strapped in, the two friends sat

staring at each other's shoes, the sack,
their hands, the banana-green sack. The pilot
sipped warm Coke and radioed the morgue.
In the cratered Strike Zone far below
smoke drifted up from a fragmented tomb.
A man burnt incense at his father's grave.

Before their clouding, before closing, one sees
oneself in the eyes of the dead,
eyes of the children cut down like skinny chickens,
eyes of the small-breasted women, wiry men.
Those who became completely wise cried out
as the slugs shattered the windshield,
glass flying into spiderwebs,
as skipping bullets slivered their eyes.
Gitelson, do-gooder? a fool?
Dead, I am your father, brother. Dead, we are your son.

Saying Goodbye to Mr. and Mrs. Mỹ, Saigon, 1972

The ancients liked to write about natural beauty.

Hồ Chí Minh, "Cảm tưởng đọc thiên gia thi"

In earlier times poets brushed on printed silk
those poems about clouds, mountains, and love.
Today, when "poems are cased in steel," poets know
that fine words only limit and lie,
that literary talk only tugs at the ear.
A poet had better keep his mouth shut, we might say,
unless he's found words to comfort and teach.
Today, comfort and teaching can also deceive
and it takes cruelty to make any friends
when it is a lie to speak, a lie to keep silent.
Wise to this, most of us still talk too much. A few
trail morning beaches studying seadrift, marveling
at curls broken bare in crushed shells,
at the sheen and cracks of laved, salted wood,
at the pearling blues of rock-stuck mussels,
each odd as friends: accidental, fragmented.

Carcanet: After Our War

For thy Carcanets of pearle, shalt thou have Carcanets of Spyders, or the greene venomous flies, Cantharides.

THOMAS NASHE, *CHRIST'S TEARES OVER JERUSALEM*

When we blighted the fields, the harvests replied:
"You have blighted your flesh." Muck-marrowed,
bones ungluing like book paste; nerve hems
shredded or grimed in something foul, leaking,
we visit each other like a plague. Kiss-Kiss.
Intelligence is helplessly evil; words lie.
Morally quits, Hieronymo gnashes off his tongue,
spits out the livid lump into a front-row lap,
but wishes, then, to explain; even to recite poetry.
Yesterday a pig snouting for truffles uncovered
moles, blind and bellyful of *Paradise Lost.*
Gleeful, let us go somewhere to curse God and die.

To market they came from land and sea, the air:
"A mighty fine place," one General agreed.
They reined in their horses and looked down to find
an old beggar woman sneaking by in their shadows.
"Call in the Doctor," barked the Seal from the Sea.
A Fourth Horseman reined up, brandishing a smile
for half the lady's face was a red, hanging bag,
one eye a wart strudel, her chin a grainy sac.
She begged. The Doctor-General offered a pin,
"My Lady, in our hour of need." He pick-pricked a node.
A yellow milk-water splashed her blouse, spurted
curdles on the Horsemen's boots, streaked to the gutter,
filled up the streets and gushed against doorsills.
The old lady cackled; the four generals beamed,
and summoned a palfrey for Their Lady to ride.

They had found Home, were Active. As they rode off
the hooves of their horses spattered the walks.

At that the fat bullets started to jump;
some whined to splice the prism of an eye. Others
bled the marrow from a rib. Windshields spidered;
the Spiders ran off, eight-legged, fast, with money,
more than you can guess, stuck to their hairy legs.
Spontaneous Generation! The Bore-Flies sang
"Every wound has two lips, so give us a kiss."
Then a two-headed cow jumped over the moon,
kicked over its lantern. Fire caught Straw.
The cow burst like a 500-lb. bomb. *Everyone*
came running—all the old folks—Slit Eye
and Spilled Guts, Fried Face and little Missy Stumps.
They plaited a daisy chain. This necklace. For you.

I believe that much unseen is also here
WALT WHITMAN, "SONG OF THE OPEN ROAD"

Lighting Out for the Territories

Afoot and light-hearted I take to the open road
WALT WHITMAN, "SONG OF THE OPEN ROAD"

In 1962, just out of high school, I drove from Philadelphia to the Seattle World's Fair with a classmate, Hans Peters Jr., in his crappy old car. Hans had also just graduated, and neither of us had any prospects or plans. Neither of us had been anywhere on our own. We told our families we could get jobs at the fair. They seemed willing to believe us and waved us good-bye, be careful.

A day or so later, somewhere in the Midwest, the car's battery started dying. Not wanting to spend our small bankroll on a new one, we kept on by leaving the engine running at gas stops and parking on hilltops at night so that when we woke to daybreak traffic, I could push-start us, with blond and lanky Hans at the wheel working the clutch and ignition as the car rolled downhill until the engine coughed, caught, varoomed with a clatter, and we were on our way again heading to the mythical West of our sixties generation. It was all new. We were on our own! Dharma bums! On the road. Free!

When we got to Seattle and its new Space Needle, we discovered there were no jobs for two kids with no real work experience. And it rained all the time. All the time. It got old fast. Now we had even less money and were sleeping in the car in our wet clothes. I decided to go home.

So I set off hitchhiking, abandoning Hans and Seattle, thumbing rides all the way back, getting picked up . . . by some sweet old folks who wanted to buy me a meal . . . by a preacher who said I could sleep in his church and offered me a tractor-driving job on a local farm . . . by a guy with heavily chained dogfighting dogs lying on the backseat in their poop . . . by three roughnecks about my own age (one with two black eyes) who were taking their driver back to Ames, Iowa, to surrender to the police . . . and once by a beautiful girl in a Volvo whom I advised not to pick up strangers.

On that long trip back across the continent I was seeing America with nothing intervening, not through its representations in magazines or movies or TV but what was really out there along its vast highways. As I would later assess it, I had pulled the shroud off my adolescent head and was seeing the Hopkinsesque "inscape" in the landscape, the "much unseen" of place and population that Whitman saw more than a hundred years before, writing

> Afoot and light-hearted I take to the open road,
> Healthy, free, the world before me,
> The long brown path before me leading wherever I choose.
> . . . .
> You road I enter upon and look around, I believe you are not
>   all that is here,
> I believe that much unseen is also here.

The next time I hitchhiked across the US was a decade later, after two trips to Vietnam. The US had changed. I had changed. The "much unseen" had also changed.

After Our War

> After our war, the dismembered bits
> —all those pierced eyes, ear slivers, jaw splinters,
> gouged lips, odd tibias, skin flaps, and toes—
> came squinting, wobbling, jabbering back.
> The genitals, of course, were the most bizarre,
> inching along roads like glowworms and slugs.
> The living wanted them back but good as new.
> The dead, of course, had no use for them.
> And the ghosts, the tens of thousands of abandoned souls
> who had appeared like swamp fog in the city streets,
> on the evening altars, and on doorsills of cratered homes,
> also had no use for the scraps and bits

because, in their opinion, they looked good without them.
Since all things naturally return to their source,
these snags and tatters arrived, with immigrant uncertainty,
in the United States. It was almost home.
So, now, one can sometimes see a friend or a famous man talking
with an extra pair of lips glued and yammering on his cheek,
and this is why handshakes are often unpleasant,
why it is better, sometimes, not to look another in the eye,
why, at your daughter's breast thickens a hard keloidal scar.
After the war, with such Cheshire cats grinning in our trees,
will the ancient tales still tell us new truths?
Will the myriad world surrender new metaphor?
After our war, how will love speak?

By then I had started teaching at Penn State and my abiding thoughts were a turmoil from far away in Saigon, where my best friends remained: Steve Erhart, who had become a reporter after working for RMK-BRJ construction, where he leaked the files on their infamous "Tiger Cage" prison; and Crystal Steinbeck, Steve's former wife, who worked at Dispatch News, who helped uncover evidence of the My Lai Massacre, and who just had a baby with John Steinbeck IV, son of the writer, all of them living together in and out of the old Graham Greene apartment on Tu Do Street, where sometimes Greene's opium pipemaster still climbed the creaky stairs with his odiferous valise to service his new American customers "chasing the dragon"—reporters like Sean Flynn and Dana Stone, now gone missing in Cambodia.

That spring, with my friends in the thick of it, the war bumbled on, and I broke my foot stealing home in a faculty–grad student baseball game, which put me in a cast and on crutches. My spring semester classes had kept me busy and focused, but they were almost over. About the time I had the cast cut off, I learned that Steve Erhart had returned to San Francisco to be operated on for stomach cancer. I resolved to go see him, perhaps to say goodbye. Perhaps it was friendship, perhaps it was just the pull of Whitman's open road, but I told my patient, newly wed wife that I needed to see America again to figure out whether I could even live in it.

So in 1974, when the spring semester ended, she dropped me off on Route 80 with an orange backpack, my crutches, and a CB walkie-talkie.

Hiking with a walkie-talkie, I would like to note, was my cultural innovation. I knew that citizens band radios were being used by truckers to talk to each other on the highways, so I figured I could use a handheld walkie-talkie to ask them for rides. No standing by the roadside holding up a barely readable sign to whatever sped by. With my walkie-talkie I could announce myself for miles down the highways. "Hi, I am standing here at mile-marker 445. I have a CB and am heading to San Francisco."

Hitchhiking and Listening to My CB Walkie-Talkie

In Questa, Chicanos shot four Anglo bikers.
Roared in on Harleys; rolled out under sheets.

In Boulder, an Indian buck-knifed a bartender.
Zigged, I guess, when he should've zagged.

At Rock Springs, my CB buzzed with double trouble;
On Friday, a cop at Green River wasted a narc.

Next night, at the Teddy Bear Inn, some girl
shot a guy through his nose. Oh, why am I in Wyoming?

At dawn in Salt Lake City, I heard swallows
chittering below a bridge as light washed the Big Dipper.

And then ol' Captain Coors was honking with that Sugarlips
about the cabbie blown away by his fare.

Outside of Reno, I was riding in a big Peterbilt
when the trucker waved a snubnose at my head.

Just to let me know, you know. He didn't shoot.
But it makes you wonder about the living and the dead.

Late at night, when radio waves skip across States,
you can hear ricochets from Maine to LA.

Story

The guy picked me up north of Santa Fe
where the red hills, dotted with piñon,
loop down from the Divide into mesas and plain.
I was standing out there—just me, my pack,
and the Gila monsters—when he hauled his Buick
off the road in a sputter of cinders and dust.
And got out, a gray-bearded, 6-foot, 300-pounder,
who stretched and said, "Do you want to drive?"
So I drove and he told me the story of his life.

How his father was a Russian Jew who got zapped
by the Mob during Prohibition, how he quit school
at fifteen and got a job as a DJ in Detroit,
how he sold flatware on the road and made a mint,
how he respected his wife, but didn't love her,
how he hit it big in radio and TV, how he fell in love,
how he found himself, at 50, in intensive care
where his wife, his kids, his girlfriend, and his rabbi
huddled in silence about his bed when his doctor
came in and whispered that maybe he ought to ask
the wife and the girlfriend to alternate visits
"because it wasn't too good for his heart."

"What about your kids?" I asked. "What do they do?"
"My daughter runs our store. My son is dead."
He studied a distant peak and didn't continue.

"What did he die of?"—"He died of suicide
. . . No, that's not right. Nixon killed him.
My son was a sweet kid, hated guns and violence

and then, during that fucking war, he hijacked a plane
and flew it to Cuba. He shot himself in Havana."
He studied the peak, then grinned and said,
"Brave little fucker, wasn't he?" I nodded.

Riding Westward

Hence is't, that I am carryed towards the West
This day, when my Soules forme bends toward the East.
JOHN DONNE, "GOODFRIDAY, 1613. RIDING WESTWARD"

You know that something's not quite right.
Perhaps the town is one of those
that marks its name and elevation
on a water tower stuck up on a hill.
Or maybe the hill itself declares the name
in whitewashed stones set just behind the town.
The big thing is the grain elevators.
The blacktop runs straight into them
just as country roads point to steeples
in Protestant towns along the Rhine.
But these tall towers are filled with wheat,
with corn and oats and rye, not hymns
to the stern father who sends us to the fields
or bids us read his Book before we eat,
who shuts our eyes in calms of beastlike sleep.

This poem is no tract for Jesus.
No fewer evils or epiphanies of joy
rise up here than did in Europe, which these
good farmers left because it was a grave.
Still, one wonders. What was all this for,
the grizzled duffer in the John Deere cap asks
as he shuffles to Main Street's secondhand sale.
Rubble of shoes in cardboard boxes. And boots,
old button boots, a pile of iron peaveys
which rolled cottonwoods down from the river,
the forest long since cleared. Cracked photos

of a jackrabbit hunt, the creatures piled high
in heaps before the log-and-sod schoolhouse.

I mean, he asks, as he tweaks his balls
through the hole in his right jean pocket,
why did they do this? What was it for?
Doves perch on a wire above the dusty road.
Swallows sweep into a storefront eave.
A clump of orange lilies closes with the day.
A CB chatters in a parked Ford truck
its back bed loaded up with bales of hay:
"We got a Kojak with a Kodak takin' pictures
. . . he done a flip-flop on the superslab."
The pickup's empty; the owner's in the bar.

The rightest place to worry all this out
is at the first dead farmhouse outside town.
Sit there on the stoop's blistered boards
as swallows chitter toward their roosts,
the fat sun sinking in reddish pollen haze
beyond the silos, beyond the tasseled fields.

Crossing West Nebraska, Looking for Blue Mountain

Where can one find the real Blue Mountain?
Inside the Blue Mountain at Waggoner's Gap,
is there another, pulsing cool azure light?
Can one drive west and find Blue Mountain?
Will anyone ever live there but me?
Some say that Blue Mountain is very small
and is rocking in the zion of a waterbead.
They claim to find it everywhere, even in clouds
of atmospheric dust snapping with strontium
and settling on the grasslands this evening.
Although Blue Mountain is only as large as a thought,
its sides drop off into dark crags; its steep slopes
are smooth as glass. Its aspect is discouraging.
But from its peak, one can see everything clearly:

In humming fields, beetles, aphids, weevils, ants.
Fox pups frisking in bluebells before their burrow.
A naked boy and girl dogpaddling an inner tube
in bayou waters, off a levee near Big Mamou.
Subterranean rocks grinding in the San Andreas Fault.
A Malay fisherman, perched on a spit of rock off Penang,
hurling a circling net into surf at sunset.
A bloated mare giving foal in a clover field in Kent.
A blindfolded teenager, shoeless, slumped against a tree
as the firing squad walks off in Montevideo.
Missiles hidden like moles in Siberian silos.
A Black man, in red cotton shirt and khaki pants, his skin
alive with protozoan welts, sipping coffee in a Congo shop.
An eel sliding through a corpse's yellowed ribs
in a Mekong swamp where frogs croak and egrets fish.

Ice sparkling the coats of hundreds of reindeer with
steaming nostrils, crossing a Lapland river under a moon.

As I pass in the dark through this sleeping town
the only creatures moving on Main Street are moths.
Spinning orbits about the lamps, they fall and die.
Their husks rustle like leaves in the fluorescent light.
Were they flying to Blue Mountain? Am I there?

Kate and Gary's Bar, Red River, New Mexico

Just over the mountains from Eagle Nest
where the glacial maw ground out a valley
and oceans of gold aspens surge around steep
boulder fields and islands of evergreens and
the collapsing ghost town where hippies hole up
you come to Red River: a string of bars
and curio shops, all pine planks and logs.
The river rattles rocks behind the town.
Farther on, toward Questa where the Rockies open
to volcanic plains, a huge gray slag heap
slides toward the river from the molybdenum mine.
The town makes no claims on eternity,
a mere moment in the granite gorge
shadowed by whistling crags and forests
beside a river carving out canyons
eating its way to the sea.

Kate's son drove me into town,
picked me up off the road from Questa,
so I had her roast beef special and a beer.
She pulled a chair from the edge of the dance floor,
watched my Adam's apple bob with beer and studied
my backpack and sleeping bag leaning by the door.

"What do you do, anyway?" she asked. "You're no drifter."
"I write poetry," I said. She smiled,
and pushed her bifocals back up her nose.
"I knew you did something like that.
Grace," she called behind the bar
to the long-legged girl setting up drinks,
"bring our friend another Coors."

Sitting on Blue Mountain, Watching the Birds Fly South and Thinking of St. Julien Ravenel Childs

*If the new is, or shall be, better, purer, braver, or higher, it will
be well. This is the tale of the old, and it is done.*

MRS. ST. JULIEN RAVENEL, *CHARLESTON: THE PLACE
AND THE PEOPLE*

In a state of hysteria, the birds flap south.
Cowbirds, grackles, blackbirds, starlings
wink through the twilight in wavering lines
which break to tumble on stubbled cornfield
and woods which shrill with manic birds.
They flutter in branches, jostle and peck,
shuffle scaly claws along the boughs; nudge,
nestle, then tuck their heads in sleep.
At dawn, the flock will rise with shrieks,
scatter up, circle, and shake themselves south.
All night, katydids will chatter in the elms
as a last cricket plies its torpid trills.

Are these birds worth a whole stanza? Sure,
they point our noses south; our hearts, to memory.
I see them beady-eyed and ragtag, carpetbagging
through bright skies, over tobacco sheds
and broken levees, foggy marshes, old rice swamps,
past Moultrie's Fort on Sullivan's Island
where his rubbery palmetto-log stockade
swallowed grapeshot, bounced back British cannon,
past Sumter nearly flooded by the Bay,
to Charleston where the Ashley and Cooper rivers
"join to form the Atlantic," to Charleston
whose citizens, "like the Chinese, eat rice
and worship ancestors," and when they die
"go to Heaven and live on Legare Street."

Over mucky creeks and glints of cotton fields
my mind flies south with these raucous birds.

To you, old duffer, dreaming always of the past . . .
of a family of painters, planters, writers:
Your grandfather was a surgeon to slaves
and invented a submarine, the *Little David,*
which shunted like a squid off the Battery,
fired once at the Yankees and retired from the war.
Your grandmother described the city's fall.
The blockade, bombardment, and burning mansions,
Charleston's streets littered with window glass
as women and slaves saved what remained.
In 1922, you soldiered in Santo Domingo.
With Marines led by a latter General Lee
you chased bandits through riverine jungles
and saved the cane crop for a New York bank.
Your own interests were burned by Sherman
in a South sundered long before your birth.
These thoughts are as near as the pack of Camels
which you smoke on your porch on drizzly afternoons
as live oaks drip with autumn rain off the ocean
and the years wash like waves on a sandbar.
Last summer you floated off Folly Beach
and took in plays and opera at Spoleto,
sporting an ancient white tuxedo
yellowed like an old magnolia bloom.
The past is large-petaled and fades slowly.

We live in a world with a simple sense of use
that doesn't include poetry and musings.
Your thoughts are useless like poetry:
the tale of the better, purer, braver, higher.
You could be my brother, as well as granddad,
for the world would count us equally useless.

But I won't turn back from writing poems
or watching birds sail past Blue Mountain,
and you can't turn away from contemplating:
malarial swamps and stacks of sugarcane,
the crumbling piazza of your Georgian house,
a bag of sutures and rusting scalpels,
cavalry hooves clattering across a trestle
then splashing off into brackish swamp.

You may wonder, reading this as rains patter
the live oak twisted and huge in your yard,
where these Yankees get all their presumption,
but I can tell, St. Julien, I can tell
by traces of indigo flowering in your thoughts
that Blue Mountain has sunk like an Atlantis
deep in your riverine, dynastic mind.

Deer Kill

The deer was down in a bed of maple leaves,
leaves dappled red, like blood, in the evening.
Grabbed the spindly hocks and heaved, rolling
the heavy doe on her back. Her eyes still clear.

Cut through the leaking web of nipples,
opening the belly like a burlap sack.
The blade's razor edge nicked her stomach bag
venting a stink of fermenting grass.

Freed the livid sheath from the red walls.
Her blood pumped out. From a severed tube.
In a scalding pool. In the great rib cage.
Heart, fatter than a hand, soapy to touch.

Pink rags of huge, shattered lungs.
Dropped liver out onto scratchy leaves.
Shook loose her stomach, bladder, and bowels.
Cleaved the pelvic ring with an ax.

Hand in the clean womb of the doe,
wet and white like chicken fat.
Threw a fist of it across the stream
rilling over stones under the chill moonlight.

Dabbed leaves in blood and stuck them to my face.
Screamed "wolf" at the moon; moon said, "man."

Chasing Out the Demons

for Tim Buckley and Tracy McCallum

A bad case. Alone in the canyon,
screaming and charging a dirtbike
at the sandstone cliffs, he squinted
behind his wire-rim glasses
as the bugs splashed green and he bucked
across cottonwood roots and rubble
at breakneck speed, on a whining bike,
skidding to stops at the canyon walls.

At night, zipped in a sleeping bag,
he squirmed like a chrysalis under the moon
while the wind searched the willows
and the creek plunked into little pools
where trout batted at fireflies.

The two Indians came in his sleep:
two ghosts, pulses of wind and moonlight,
squatting beside him on the balls of their feet.
He shouted when the woman smoothed his hair.
And then they were gone and he cried.
Sobbed hard because it was goodbye,
goodbye to the spirit that raged in him by day
and now was traveling across the canyon creek
led off by the ghosts of two Indians
who had come to calm him.

He sat up that night by the dark cold water,
wrapped in a blanket, listening to the creek,
breaking his reverie only once
to cup his hands and draw to his lips
the moon rocking on the clear water.

Journey in the Desert

All evening, below a sprig of yarrow,
by creekwater tumbling through willow roots,
a cricket preened its song in the yard.
Near whirligigs spinning in a pool,
a fox paused from lapping up water
to lift his delicate paw and scratch
at red mites itching the root of his ear.
A gray millipede wiggled out from a rock.
A wind puffed in from the west as the sun
set in a stand of elms. A blackbird
bobbed off a willow switch up to a roost.
All evening crickets called. At morning, I left,

riding the interstates west, motoring past
the cauldrons of Pittsburgh, the choked air,
past HoJos, Exxons, Arbys, Gulfs,
in the yammer and slam, the drone of trucks,
past the little lives that always are there:
locusts chirring oak tops in a Tennessee graveyard,
past sawgrass and creepers, then yucca and sage,
past armadillos scuttling off the berm
—all the while listening to crickets singing
on roadsides ticking with summer heat,
in leaves that rustle in the opened hands,
in the tree that roots deep in the heart.

2. THE STONE LIONS

Surging the walls of the winding creek canyon
the old river shaved a smooth face in the stone:

pink lava; each bubble a cave; each cave, a pueblo.
Crows, railing at humans for thousands of years,
circled the tourists scaling long ladders,
poking down kivas, where Indians once sat like moles
and invited the earth to feed Spirit and Bone.
High above on the opposite cliff, a trail turns off
crossing the mesa through scraggly piñon
toward canyons too fickle with water for maize.
At Alamo Canyon, a drop and a Park sign:

> You are on the rim of Alamo Canyon. The
> Canyon here is 400 ft. deep. You should
> not cross unless you have: 1. at least
> one pint of water per person, 2. sturdy
> boots and a hat to protect you from the
> sun, and 3. better than average health.

Some miles farther on lies a ruined pueblo,
now crumbled adobe and cairns of rocks,
shards, chips of obsidian, all crowned by cactus.
Nearby is a ring of great, raised-up stones
with a gate so that spirits may gather and go.
In the center, a pair of carved lions crouch,
bellies in dust, always ready to leap,
but corralled by a hedge of bleached antler prongs.
Flint-bits and shards have been cast to the lions.
The arrow shall fly and the cup brim water.

3. KACHINA

Canyons, mesas, buttes and chaparral.
A place so dry a cough can start a cloud;
terrain so odd, without events or acts,
a rock or circling crow might seem a sign,
a sheet of rain escorted by the sun

moves like a girl, sent by gods to dance,
whose beaded skirt of raindrops shot with light
will brush the canyon walls and fill up pools
thrilling songbirds thirsting in the dust.
Sheltered in a cave, I watch her pass
and wonder who and why and where she's gone;
and doubt, as in our lives or with a love,
if what I've seen and felt took place at all.
But trust these dripping leaves and trickling spells,
the human augured in the magpie's splash.

4. AT CAPULIN CANYON

Night fell deep in the chilled-off canyon;
birds rustled in willows and oaks; were hushed
by the little creek's loudening chatter and rill.

Hidden in a cove of cottonwoods, I dozed
while sprinkles of stars circled the Pole Star.
The moon lifted over the eastern cliff wall.

The wind sailed in the tops of the pines.
Later, a snort and the stamping of hooves
startled me up as some great beast
crashed through the creek in a clatter of stones.

At daybreak, I spotted a lone horse grazing
in dry chaparral. I stalked the big stallion.
His coat slate gray. Dusted white. He stared,

flicked ears at my whistle, then galloped off
pounding up pumice at the caldera rim.
Coronado, Lame Dog, Two Moons, Price,
your revenant horse is lost in arroyos.

5. PAINTED CAVE

And new Philosophy calls all in doubt.

JOHN DONNE, "THE FIRST ANNIVERSARY"

Not really a cave, but, as Bandelier said,
"a grand portal of volcanic tuff,"
a massive vault in the basalt cliff
overlooking a wide canyon floor, strewn
with pocked boulders, a broken lava flow,
spiny cholla cactus, and stunted junipers.
And here Indians cut a ladder in the stone
to paint a roof with worries of their world:
the Spaniards' church at Santa Fe, a cross,
a bell, an armored man, horses, deer,
Indians striding with woven shields,
a bucket-headed god with a bird's blank eyes.
Were these paintings spiritual complaint?
Sad attempts to rule a hostile place?
And if their world was broken by greater force,
what can we say of ours: pulled into empty space
where galaxies writhe in igneous fury
to produce a living cell as part, their part,
of an elaborate practical joke.

The conquistadors have fallen from their mounts
and wander these wastes in search of water.
And if the desert gods loaned them a cave,
what would they paint? A plane, a clock,
blank sky, empty sea, the stalking atomic ghost.

6. WEDDING IN THE DESERT

A huge curtain of cloud torn down
spilling rain and sunfall into the desert

onto a horned toad squatting with bald eye
near a fishhook cactus. The bright droplets
stutter in the dust by its head. It blinks.
High above, out of the lip of light cascading
from the raincloud, a man is falling,
smaller than a gnat, falling through the skylight,
swelling enormously as he tumbles to earth
to alight on the mesa, the bare mesa
where at night a blue lamp is always burning.

— —

Toward dawn, two nimbus clouds drifted in,
the larger—trailing down tendrils of rain
like a Portuguese man-o'-war—began to pulse
with lightning, brightening its belly
like a huge lantern, arcing a jagged streak
to ignite the smaller cloud.
Pulsing and flaring, striking each other,
dragging the earth with rain,
they drifted off over the mountains.
All about them the sky was clear.

The Gift of Morning Water

After the long night with a cold wind riffling the scrim of the teepee lit like a lantern on the deserted prairie, a night of chills in the small of the back, aches in crossed legs, after all the hours of chanting from Indians and Anglos, after their drumming on the iron kettle stretched with hide, its water-filled belly bellowing when tipped, after the prayers sung for forgiveness, for guidance from the grandfather peyote on the crescent of sand, after chewing bitter buttons, swallowing dry powder, after the drumming and the singing and the sweet sage thrown on the dazzling fire, as the embers died and dawn finally rinsed the top of the tent, the Road Chief, an elderly Tiwa who throughout the night had asked "him" to show us the right road, said: "A woman is coming with morning water. Listen to her. She is your mother."

An old Pueblo woman crawled through the tent flap, short of breath and shoving before her on the teepee sand a steel bucket, water sloshing, ladle clanking, and I turned with exhaustion, with disappointment, for all night long I had sat eating the "medicine," going out only once under the huge, roaring stars to take a leak and return, and nothing, really, had happened.

And then she spoke with puffy, tired lips, said, "You have done a good thing here tonight. Drink this water and be refreshed," and every syllable that came from her was perfectly the voice of my own mother, dead for many years. Stunned, and now weeping, I sat as the bucket came around to me, wept hard at hearing her voice again.

I have a friend in Vermont who, for a full week after his father's death, kept calling the family answering machine, just to hold a bit longer to his father's voice. And here I was made a gift I hadn't known how much I wanted, the voice that called my name the first morning of my life.

Peyote Villanelle

Watch out for this one, USA.
PEYOTE ROAD CHIEF, TAOS, NM

I

The trail lost, he looked about
across the bouldered canyon floor.
In desert wastes the soul cries out

then echoes back in dusty shouts,
wavering ghosts in chaparral.
The trail lost, he looked about

the creekbed where he shot his mount.
Horseflies sucked the splash of gore.
In desert wastes the soul cries out.

Though no one heard, he called out loud.
Snakes uncurled in a cave's cool door.
The trail lost, he looked about

and shuffled forth, dry in mouth,
aching for home and green remorro.
In desert wastes the soul cries out

in blind canyons, under blank sky. Scouting
for water, throat parched and sore,
with the trail lost he looked about
desert wastes. The soul cries out.

2

"Come eat peyote and you shall live."
The woman waved and called him on.
"A god has made this road a gift."

She crossed the arroyo and came to him
cloaked in light and shakes of rain.
"Come, eat peyote and you shall live."

Her fingers brushed his blistered lips.
She talked like water; touched like dawn.
A god had made the road a gift.

for in that realm of scorpion and snake
his soul cried out and the woman came
fashioned from light and veiled in rain.
He followed a god through desert wastes.

Heading out West

All evening, below a sprig of yarrow,
by creekwater plunging through willow roots,
a cricket preened its song in our yard.

Down by the back eddy spinning with whirligigs,
I watched a fox pause from lapping up water
to lift a delicate paw and scratch
at red mites itching the root of its ear.

Then, as the sun ignited the willow stand
a blackbird flapped off a branch,
crossing shadowy fields like a thought.

All evening as crickets called, I creaked
a rocker on our paint-peeled porch,
sipped whiskey, watched mist and fireflies
fill up the meadow, and considered
—long before I was a father—
my fellow Americans, the funny business of being married,
my deadly job and the jobs that would follow,
and all I could think of as I sat there
—safe from harm, steadily employed, happily married—
was how to get away.

         At morning, I left,
hopping a ride west on the interstate, past
the cauldrons of Pittsburgh, its choked air,
past Hojos, Exxons, Arbys, Gulfs,
in the yammer and slam, the drone of trucks,
past the little lives that always are there,
past locusts chirring in a Tennessee graveyard,

past kudzu, pecans, then yucca and sage,
past armadillos scuttling off the berm of the highway,
. . . all the while wondering just what I was doing,
not sure where I was going; less sure, why.
But standing there, hanging out my thumb,
squinting at the stream of oncoming cars.

Daddy out Hitchhiking at 3:00 a.m.

Finally it was just me, and the katydids
cranking out nightsongs in clumps of willows
by a barn roofed in moonlight, by a ryefield
luminous with dew. I stepped off the highway
ribboning out through the valley. Walked
through wet weeds to a pond gathering vapors.

Angels see the way I saw that night
when only large shapes loomed
and all my thoughts were laid aside
as I searched the night opening before me
and soul shuffled out of self to sing
with katydids chattering in murky trees.

All beasts are kind with divine instruction.
The paired ducks slept beneath their wings.
Minnows wavered in the moon-charmed creek
where a muskrat hunched and licked its paws
listening like me to insects calling
searching and calling at the end of summer.

This is what Daddy was doing
the August you were born.
Wandering off alone on highways
walking off highways into the night
calming a head loud with the past
listening to things that make a song.

Words for My Daughter

About eight of us were nailing up forts
in the mulberry grove behind Reds's house
when his mother started screeching and
all of us froze except Reds—fourteen, huge
as a hippo—who sprang out of the tree so fast
the branch nearly bobbed me off. So fast,
he hit the ground running, hammer in hand,
and seconds after he got in the house
we heard thumps like someone beating a tire
off a rim   his dad's howls   the screen door
banging open   Saw   Reds barreling out
through the tall weeds toward the highway
the father stumbling after his fat son
who never looked back across the thick swale
of teazel and black-eyed susans until it was safe
to yell fuck you at the skinny drunk
stamping around barefoot and holding his ribs.

Another time, the Connelly kid came home to find
his alcoholic mother getting raped by the milkman.
Bobby broke a milk bottle and jabbed the guy
humping on his mom. I think it really happened
because none of us would loosely mention that
wraith of a woman who slippered around her house
and never talked to anyone, not even her kids.
Once a girl ran past my porch
with a dart in her back, her open mouth
pumping like a guppy's, her eyes wild.
Later that summer, or maybe the next,
the kids hung her brother from an oak.
Before they hoisted him, yowling and heavy

on the clothesline, they made him claw the creekbank
and eat worms. I don't know why his neck didn't snap.

Reds had another nickname you couldn't say
or he'd beat you up: "Honeybun."
His dad called him that when Reds was little.

— —

So, these were my playmates. I love them still
for their justice and valor and desperate loves
twisted in shapes of hammer and shard.
I want you to know about their pain
and about the pain they could loose on others.
If you're reading this, I hope you will think,
Well, my Dad had it rough as a kid, so what?
If you're reading this, you can read the news
and you know that children suffer worse.

— —

Worse for me is a cloud of memories
still drifting off the South China Sea,
like the 9-year-old boy, naked and lacerated,
thrashing in his pee on a steel operating table
and yelling "*Đau. Đau,*" while I, trying to translate
in the mayhem of Tet for surgeons who didn't know
who this boy was or what happened to him, kept asking
"Where? Where's the pain?" until a surgeon
said "Forget it. His ears are blown."

— —

I remember your first Halloween
when I held you on my chest and rocked you,
so small your toes didn't touch my lap
as I smelled your fragrant peony head
and cried because I was so happy and because

I heard, in no metaphorical way, the awful chorus
of Sœur Anicet's orphans writhing in their cribs.
Then the doorbell rang and a tiny Green Beret
was saying trick-or-treat and I thought *oh oh*
but remembered it was Halloween and where I was.
I smiled at the evil midget, his map-light and night paint,
his toy knife for slitting throats, said,
"How ya doin', soldier?" and, still holding you asleep
in my arms, gave him a Mars bar. To his father
waiting outside in fatigues I hissed, "You shit,"
and saw us, child, in a pose I know too well.

I want you to know the worst and be free from it.
I want you to know the worst and still find good.
Day by day, as you play nearby or laugh
with the ladies at Peoples Bank as we go around town
and I find myself beaming like a fool,
I suspect I am here less for your protection
than you are here for mine, as if you were sent
to call me back into our helpless tribe.

Agua Fría y Las Chicharras

1. ALHAMBRA

When the voice of the Prophet crossed the Sahara
clattering out from mud-walled souks with Berber horsemen,
it carried swiftly through those wastes, for as the Arabs say,
in the desert there is nothing but the presence of Allah.
And in Granada, below snow peaks rinsing in sunlight,
at the Alhambra, Al Qal'a al-Hamra, the Architect's Garden,
the Moors made Him visible everywhere, in horseshoe portals
and sandstone ramparts stamped with the Key,
in icy fountains teased out from the rock
looping toward heaven, collapsing in pools, plunging down
stairwells banistered in liquid light. *¿Quién quiere agua?*
the water-carriers sang, *agua más fría que nieve.*
In the spill of water, the signature of god.
And outside the citadel of Allah, in paradisiacal parks,
the locusts calling at the edge of wilderness.

2. ARROYO HONDO, NEW MEXICO

He pitched his camp inside a canyon
where willows twist on boulders shoved up beside the creek.
Poplars shook out sunlight after a rain. By the dead fire
lay a charred bean can and a plastic bag spilling out flour.
In the creek, a Coors six-pack; a pint of half-and-half.
He had some clothes draping a rock, a bedroll
sprawled on soggy blankets. By that, an empty suitcase.
I found him staring at the stream.
He looked about thirty, said he lived near Denver,
put up sheetrock for a living, was leaving for LA.
He said he had been to her place in town. It was empty.
He stood outside her house until he heard echoes gather,

saw shapes move, imagined her children's yelps,
her laughter, her husband's arms around her
as they leaned against the sink and kissed.
The marigolds she left behind still glimmered in the shade
below the cottonwood where, high up, locusts called.
He said it was like he saw her reading by the window
then putting down the book to stare at him staring in.
Like a ghost watching a ghost. He offered me a beer
saying he had come here through a valley of lies
with no guide but hunger for her. No Christ, no cop, no book,
no mother or father, no flag, and the few friends he counted
were gone and God knows where. She too was gone for good.
He wanted me to know about a lake,
dry, some sixty miles up north in Colorado
where Indians emerged as men, led out, led up
from Sipapu, the Underworld, upon pulses of song
by Kokopelli, the Hump-Backed Flute Player, the Locust God,
whose song can heal. We sipped his beer and listened
to whines of locusts falling on the creek.

3. ROSALE'S

Ro-*sáh*-le's. Just north of Taos in El Prado
past the feed sign for henscratch: $5.50/50 lbs.
You go there if you're hungry and it's late.
Rosale's a Mexican from Juárez, does a big business
from midnight to dawn when all the drunks
and lounge lizards stumble in as bars shut down.

So everyone's ugly and stiff in the eye sockets
because it's too late to get laid, because
their lives stink. So they fight.
Once the cops raided and took away a lot of guns
but I never heard of anyone *dying* there
so I go . . . and one night I saw an awful fight

with four drunks kicking this squirmy Anglo
who had been coldcocked while eating his eggs
and lay groaning below a table, everyone just watching
until the big girl in the blue smock waddled out
from the kitchen, screamed, and shoved them out.
No fun in that fight at all.

When I left, dawn was cracking behind the mountains
and high up I saw the bright porpoise brow of a jet
streaming east, nose silvery with sunlight
above the darkened earth. The plane was a comfort
darting across the open sky like a clear thought,
it said, "Look around. The signs are all about you
even in a sorry brawl in a Mexican café."
Each spring, I thought, they clean the ditches,
the *acequias,* of leaf muck and debris.
Each must marvel when waters spill again
and cottonwoods shimmer in a web of poems
as redwings bob and whistle the branches
and canyons fill with the locust's song.
Oh, the hunger for words pure as clear water
that shall slake the pain of our parched tongues
and, splashed against our brows, shall let us see.
In such a moment, locusts reinstruct our rapture.
Cold and mute, we are led up from dark worlds
into a sunstruck glade loud with rilling water.
At the song's start, the raw tongue stammers out
an urge toward paradise, a version of ease.

Some Things That Happened before Our Daughter's Birth

I. A POEM HER MOTHER WROTE ME THE YEAR I WAS AWAY

Snow piles up these lonely nights.
This winter you are gone.
Knee-deep, February drifts choke
the railroad bed we walked in summer
edged by daisys and black-eyed susans.

From the woods Rangers drag out deer.
Ribs poke through their rusty coats.
The Rangers say "no food." Too much snow.
The coldest winter in our century.

Fitting that we should be apart.
Powerful winds and hibernation of the soul.
Like the deer pawing for bark, I peel away
the crust of my own heart, pumping these days
in a white expanse, frozen every dawn,
as snow falls where we walked together.

2. MY REPLY

Sweetest love, I do not go
For weariness of thee . . .
                        JOHN DONNE

Let's say that I was called away
summoned by a voice I heard first as a boy
when belly down on the cool bank
I looked in the wrinkling water
at skeeters sculling tiny oars,
at a crayfish wading through willow roots
unraveling under clear ripples.
I was so still a woodthrush supped beside me.
So quiet, I dwelt with spotted newts.

"Come" is all that voice has ever said,
wet with ferns and mossy logs
with catbird cry and frog croak.
And when I followed I was always happy
reading delight in signatures of fish,
in moth glyphs scribbled beneath elm bark,
even though lonely; as now, for you.

What calls me away shall call me home.
I knew your voice before we met.
These journeys out, are journeys back.
Let's say my travels tend toward you.

Snowbound

Tragedies of clouds still stumble over us
stalled in cars and tractor trailers
along the highway blocked at a mountain pass,
but now a track team from a chartered bus
has shoved a van past a jackknifed trailer
and so, after long hours, a lane is cleared
for all the bickering parents and bratty kids
for truckers zonked on speed and nattering on CBs
for the long-hauler with straggly hair and no front teeth
who struck out in the snow to straighten things out
and stomped back angry, and for the snoozing salesmen,
for the old folks too shy to pee by the road
for the teenagers yelling in hormonal fits
for the wailing babies, for the diabetic
shooting his thigh behind a fogged windshield
for the lovers feeling lucky at being trapped together
and, oh, just wishing it were night,
for all of us now inching forward in a glittering line
resuming our lives under sweeps of clearing sky.

Passing through Albuquerque

At dusk, by the irrigation ditch
gurgling past backyards near the highway,
locusts raise a maze of calls in cottonwoods.

A Spanish girl in a white party dress
strolls the levee by the muddy water
where her small sister plunks in stones.

Beyond a low adobe wall and a wrecked car
men are pitching horseshoes in a dusty lot.
Someone shouts as he clangs in a ringer.

Big winds buffet in ahead of a storm,
rocking the immense trees and whipping up
clouds of dust, wild leaves, and cottonwool.

In the moment when the locusts pause and the girl
presses her up-fluttering dress to her bony knees
you can hear a banjo, guitar, and fiddle

playing "The Mississippi Sawyer" inside a shack.
Moments like that, you can love this country.

The proper subjects for poetry are love, virtue, and war.
DANTE, *DE VULGARI ELOQUENTIA*, BK. 2

Fun with Tom and Jane

As the war droned on, my wife's Saigon university finally paid her salary after we threatened a lawsuit, paying her all at once at the end of the school year in so many packets of devalued piasters that we had to carry it away in two suitcases, making our motorcycle trip back to our apartment a bit tricky as we squeezed through the city traffic with our luggage on our little Honda 50. A large part of that money, as well as my own Hué University salary, we would soon give away in the rain one night the next week, in Hué, where it was our exhausting bad luck to be there as it seemed about to fall once again to the regular North Vietnamese Army, which had now routed the Saigon troops north of the city on Easter, 1972.

We had come on one last trip to see the imperial tombs and the old royal city. That day, as we walked the monuments with Vietnamese friends, the aerial and sea bombing started thudding again into the distant mountains, and by evening, as heavy rains fell, the minority tribes who lived in those mountains had to flee their homes and go to the city for shelter. Whole families, whole clans—barefooted men, nursing mothers, toddlers, and bent grandparents—had left their ancestral villages to escape the bombs and were walking into Hué in their single-file style. Moi, the Vietnamese called them, "savages." We doubted they'd even be given shelter from the rain. Holding a pistol under my poncho, I stood by as my recently married, twenty-two-year-old wife, just out of college, gave away our money in the drumming downpour, returning several times to take more packets of cash from my satchel and weeping as she told me about one old man who did not even seem to know what she was handing him. For us, it was play money. We were going home.

REMEMBERING HEAVEN'S FACE, CHAPTER 21

Our new home was at a country crossroads called Warriors Mark, just over a long mountain running east from Port Matilda, Pennsylvania. Sitting on a hill, surrounded by tilled fields, our old farmhouse lay at the end of a gravel lane bordered by scrubby trees and blackberry bushes and edged by fields plowed and spread with lime, soon to sprout horse corn, blond sweeps of barley, or tassels of sorghum. On a tangly slope off one side of the house, a little creek rippled through willows on its way down to

Gatesburg Road, where it flowed under a bridge and down past a chicken farm. Standing on our creaky wooden porch and looking west over the creek and across a field gone to hay, you could see our only other neighbor . . . a small white church with a belfry and graveyard, perched on a hill under cedars and rarely used. Our green valley was wonderfully quiet, our summer evenings murmuring with crickets and the creek.

The house was not in bad shape even though it had been left empty for quite a while. We rented it from a wealthy farmer a valley away, where his family managed a large dairy farm. Actually, there were two houses on our rental. Face-to-face with ours was the other, now empty one, along with its abandoned chicken coop and a goat pen. We had adopted a dog from the local pound, a sort of russet-colored collie, that Lonnie named Apples. Apples liked to show her stuff by barking when deer slipped out of the woods above our house to graze in the fields in the evening.

We were a world away from Vietnam, where just a few months before, in Huế, at night, in a drumming downpour, I had stood by, holding a pistol under my hooded poncho, as Lonnie gave away all our piasters to a long line of refugees fleeing the bombing in the mountains nearby. Now her long, blonde, hippie-girl hair was cut short for her graduate program at Penn State, where I taught freshman comp and something called "college grammar." The commute, a half-hour drive, took us through the State Game Lands at Scotia, turned onto the highway at Carson's gas station, then into town, past trailer parks and repair shops, a hardware store, a Dunkin' Donuts, a liquor store, then the tree-lined streets with faculty homes, and finally the big, sprawling campus of brick buildings. Vietnam was behind us. After my years there evacuating war-injured children to hospital care, and then Lonnie's miscarriage in Saigon, we'd had enough of it. The war was on the news, sure, and the campus was sometimes in turmoil as the war dragged on, but for us, it was over.

But not quite.

One day I got a call from someone who said she was from the Indochina Peace Campaign and would we consider taking in Jane Fonda when she spoke at Penn State in a few weeks? She would be traveling with a few others from the IPC and they needed a place to stay, away from public scrutiny. Someone—she never said who—had recommended us. Did I think my place would be safe and secure? I said I would talk to my wife and get back to her.

The Indochina Peace Campaign was a kind of anti–Bob Hope/USO traveling roadshow of skits and songs and speeches with an anti-war message, all thrown together in the wake of the Chicago mayhem and the trial of the Chicago Seven. In 1971, the IPC produced a movie with Fonda and Donald Sutherland, along with singer Holly Near, called *F.T.A.*—letters one sometimes saw in Vietnam scrawled on latrine stall walls: Fuck the Army. The IPC, when questioned by the press, said FTA stood for "Free the Army."

Fonda apparently had been invited to speak at Penn State. The IPC roadshow that she traveled with was headed elsewhere after her talk. The security question was a real one because she'd been receiving death threats since her trip to Hanoi and that notorious photo of her sitting on a North Vietnamese antiaircraft battery along with smiling NVA gunners in pith helmets.

We thought a bit and called back. Yes, we could put them up.

And then we got nervous. We just didn't want to hear any more rhetorical posturing about the war, and the IPC was proposing that Tom Hayden would also be coming, along with others from the Indochina Peace Campaign. Hayden, I knew, was the author of the Port Huron Statement and a founder of SDS. We didn't yet know that Hayden and Fonda were a couple. Neither of them were very popular with Middle America or here in the middle of Pennsylvania. And, as I said, neither Lonnie nor I was up for hearing any lectures about Vietnam. Anyway, where would we put everyone? What were we thinking? Our farmhouse had two bedrooms and a single bathroom upstairs. A pullout couch downstairs. How were Lonnie and I going to handle a Hollywood princess, her inflammatory friend, and their coterie of agitators? At that time, I preferred my agitation done solo, no megaphone.

We needed some backup. Lonnie suggested we could use the house across from us. So I got on the phone and invited our friends from Vietnam for whom the war was not a political abstraction but who, like us, actually lived there during the conflict: John Steinbeck IV, also just back, his wife, Crystal, and their toddler, Blake (born in Saigon), and with them,

Louise Stone, whose CBS photographer husband, Dana, was still listed as missing in Cambodia, along with his photographer friend Sean Flynn (the actor's son), both having been captured but not yet declared dead. The Steinbecks and Stone were now living together in an apartment on Morton Street in New York and had a standing invitation to visit us in Warriors Mark. All of us were adjusting to living in the US as its war dragged on. Louise, dedicated to finding her missing husband and Flynn, was staying with John and Crystal while working in New York with Walter Cronkite and his group of journalists (the US Committee to Free Journalists Held in Southeast Asia). A year earlier, Richard Avedon had taken a soulful photo of Louise to help advertise her search. People got quiet and listened when Louise spoke in her own quiet way. And Steinbeck, well, had bluster enough to deflate any self-important entourage. He grew up on it. His father's Nobel Laureate citation sat on the mantel at his stepmother's apartment in New York City, and when John and his brother, Tom, went off to serve in Vietnam, they first went with their father to meet President Lyndon Johnson at the White House . . . for a photo op that ran in all the papers. And Crystal, who had worked for Dispatch News in Saigon, helped break the My Lai Massacre story. Lonnie and I figured that together with our friends, we could hold our own with Tom and Jane and the IPC.

In fact, we didn't need to. A few days after our friends drove in from New York, Tom and Jane and five others from the IPC rolled in. As a caution against all their cars being noticed from the roads across the fields, I had some of them park by the far side of the empty house. That house, which now had its water turned on, was where the IPC group dropped their sleeping bags as we showed Tom and Jane their bedroom next to ours in the main house.

That first afternoon, while some of the group played Frisbee and others took walks, Lonnie and Crystal and Louise got dinner going while I played host with wine and beer. Little Blake and Apples were making friends in the kitchen—judging by the exchange of hugs for doggy face-licks down there by our knees in toddler-dog world—when Jane called down the stairs asking if Lonnie had grapefruit, as Jane was on a diet that required grapefruit for breakfast. Out in the front room, someone, maybe John, had Stevie Wonder on the record player singing "He's Misstra Know-It-All."

We all gathered in the evening after dinner. Steinbeck held forth for a while, a little tipsy after he and Louise discovered our liquor cabinet in the late afternoon and finished off a bottle of Michter's small-batch bourbon, given me as a goodbye present by a doctor I worked for in Vietnam. During Steinbeck's Vietnam army career, his job was to set up TV stations in village markets. Discharged, he returned to Saigon, where he and Crystal took up residence in the old Graham Greene apartment, moving back and forth to Phoenix Island on the Mekong near My Tho, where they became followers of the Venerable Nguyễn Thành Nam, Ông Đạo Dừa, "The Coconut Monk." That evening, the IPC group listened as John, wearing his monk's clothes, talked about the Third Force in Vietnam and his march with the frail Venerable to the US embassy in Saigon, causing a street demonstration and a scuffle between the national police—dubbed "the White Mice"— and the gathered reporters, with the cops busting cameras and yanking out film, all in front of the embassy, now in lockdown.

Jane asked me questions about my work with war-injured children. On her IPC tour, she talked about civilian casualties, and she wanted some reliable facts. I told her about my recent testimony on civilian casualties published in the proceedings of the Senate Judiciary Committee. I talked about our last year in Vietnam . . . about collecting *ca dao* folk poetry on tape, and I sang one of the folk songs that I had recently recorded in the countryside. To everyone's delight, she sang back a Vietnamese song she had learned in Hanoi. I was struck by a surprising self-effacement when she spoke and, of course, by her good looks.

She asked Lonnie what she did while I was out in the countryside on my project.

"Teaching," Lonnie said, looking up from Blake on the floor, where she was pulling Apples's tail. "Teaching English at the university in Saigon. I taught something like four hundred students."

"What was *that* like?" Jane asked, now genuinely curious.

"*Desperate.* A lot of them were soldiers desperate to become interpreters so they could get away from the fighting. Some came to class on motor-cycles—sometimes two or three riding into the courtyard on a bike, along with their weapons. I had to ask them to stack their rifles outside on the classroom porch."

Jane asked nothing more, but I could see her repicturing Lonnie, so young and pretty and just recently graduated from a university herself.

Tom Hayden stayed pretty quiet that evening. Ten years earlier, he had been jailed as a Freedom Rider in Georgia. That was the same year he composed the Port Huron Statement for SDS adoption, summoning our generation to active and direct engagement in "participatory democracy." In October 1960, Hayden—then a young reporter for the University of Michigan student newspaper—managed to meet the Kennedy brothers, handing John Kennedy a proposal for creating a Peace Corps, which Kennedy formally proposed a short time later in a speech in California. Back then, our generation thought we heard the tone of things to come in JFK's 1961 inaugural address:

> We dare not forget today that we are the heirs of that first revolution. Let the word go forth from this time and place, to friend and foe alike, that the torch has been passed to a new generation of Americans, born in this century, tempered by war, disciplined by a hard and bitter peace, proud of our ancient heritage, and unwilling to witness or permit the slow undoing of those human rights to which this nation has always been committed, and to which we are committed today at home and around the world.

But then came the Kennedy assassinations, the Vietnam War, Nixon's presidency, and, as we gathered at the farmhouse with the Indochina Peace Campaign, Watergate. The war dragged on endlessly, and Hayden became known as a key defendant in the famous Chicago Seven trial. One had the sense that his visit with us, and perhaps other visits with the IPC and other public platforms, were just stops for him along a bigger road map.

That night, after everyone pitched in to clean up the kitchen, the IPC folks went over to the other farmhouse and we went upstairs to our bedrooms—Jane and Tom to the one we saved for them next to ours, while John, Crystal, Blake, and Louise settled into their sleeping bags on the floor at the foot of our bed with Apples.

When all was quiet and we were finally drifting off, Blake, almost asleep, started crying. Crystal tried to hush and comfort her. Then John stirred from his boozy sleep, shouting, "For Christ's sake, Blake, go to sleep. What do you want? You got Apples here and fucking Jane Fonda in the next room!"

The next morning, Lonnie laid out a breakfast in the dining room, which looked down to the creek and across the field to the ever-empty hilltop church across the road. She had gotten the grapefruit for Jane. Tom was up early and out on the front lawn in baggy gym clothes doing karate exercises. Someone from the IPC contingent was already on the phone about their next stops.

Jane's talk on the Penn State campus was that evening. She was sure to have an audience. But which audience? Her recent Hanoi antiaircraft photo had outraged many across the US. Would angry vets show up? Someone with a handgun? For others, she was an immensely popular young actress whose recent movies had been nominated for Academy Awards—*They Shoot Horses, Don't They?* in 1969 and *Klute,* for which she won Best Actress in 1972. I was to chauffeur her to campus since I had a faculty ID and knew the place. I called campus security to let them know what was happening and give them the license plate for my car so it could be parked illegally at the back of Schwab Auditorium.

If Jane ever seemed hesitant in person, once she got on stage she had nerves of steel. Not me. I was full of worry about ugly or even violent behavior that might come from the audience. And then there was my job. At the time, I was a mere instructor, not even on the tenure track. My job could be gone in a blast of bad PR.

I was watching Jane from the curtained stage wings when a campus cop brought over to me a young man—clean-cut, maybe in his thirties—who was insisting he was a personal friend of hers. I don't know why the cop even let him backstage, except that the guy was very convincing about his friendship. Jane was now seated onstage at a small table with a microphone, doing Q&A with the audience. Since I didn't want to kick out someone who might actually be her friend, I had him write his name on a slip of paper and told the cop to stay with him as I went on stage with the slip. Over his name I had written, "DO YOU KNOW THIS GUY?" Jane, covering the microphone with one hand, looked at the slip and then back at me. She shook her head wearily and said, "No." I signaled the cop to usher the guy away.

And that was pretty much it. As Jane rose from her chair to immense applause, some of the IPC group moved up to the stage from their front-row seats, and all of us soon got out of there together and out to our cars, probably disappointing those who wanted to see her up close, or talk with her, or perhaps just get an autograph.

A local paper covered her talk:

JANE FONDA VISITS U.P. UNIVERSITY PARK (APS)

Calling for an immediate end to US involvement in Indochina, anti-war activist Jane Fonda, speaking to an estimated crowd of 5,000 last week, said the United States, "is waging a cultural and ecological genocide on the people of Vietnam."

The noted actress, speaking on behalf of the Indochina Peace Campaign, stated that the US policy of saturation bombing and the use of various methods of defoliation has, "raped the land of its life sustaining elements and has driven the people from their ancient ancestral homes . . . B-52s flying at 30,000 feet drop 90 tons of bombs on an area one-half mile wide by one and one-quarter miles long, wiping everything in that area off the face of the earth."

The next day, the Indochina Peace Campaign pulled out and moved on to its next venue. I think the group lasted about another year. In any case, once again our house on a hill by a country crossroads was quiet. We never saw Jane Fonda again, although I did write her and ask whether she would write a blurb for the back cover of my *Ca Dao Vietnam: A Bilingual Anthology of Vietnamese Folk Poetry*. She wrote back from Santa Monica with the following:

> "*Ca Dao Vietnam* gives us a glimpse to know the Vietnamese people in a new way." —Jane Fonda.

Back at our old farmhouse over the next few years, we raised chickens (escapees from the chicken farm down at the end of our driveway), two goats (I forget how we got them or why), and also a pair of mean geese that would peek in our porch windows and peck the bumpers of our car when we pulled up.

Other than the geese, there was never any trouble at our place, although a few times I had to chase off hunters during deer season, and once I phoned a game warden to come out to look at a deer that I had hung from a tree near the house, having dressed it out after it ran into our old Volkswagen microbus the night before as we drove home through the Scotia Game Lands. The doe was perfectly healthy, except its two back legs snapped at the joints when it hit us headfirst and bounced back. It kept trying to stand up and run off, its back legs useless. Again and again. It was horrible. I found a rock by the roadside and bashed its head. Then we opened the back of the van and shoved in the huge, dead animal, which I couldn't see leaving to rot by the road. Somehow, to my mind, this would have made the whole thing worse. That next day, the game warden told us if we had left it there, he would have found it and taken it to the kitchen at a nearby state home for children.

"What are you going to do with it?" he asked, looking us over, two youngsters living way out in the country. Hippies, maybe.

"Well, eat it," I said.

He studied it, gutted and hanging from the tree, and left it with us, walking away and saying, "Next time, leave it."

And once the landlord came by, acting odd and hesitant. He was a big man and graying. Sometimes I would drive over to his dairy farm to hand him our monthly check if we had forgotten to mail it on time. But he had never come over to our place.

"What the hell did you do to the creek?" he blurted out.

"Huh?"

"The creek is flooding," Mr. Barr said. "Did you dam it up?"

I hadn't been down to the creek for a while, so I didn't know that the field between Half Moon Creek and the church had indeed flooded a bit. We went down to the creek to take a look.

That got us a laugh together. The creek now had a little pond. Beavers, building a new lodge, had moved in and started a dam, a dam that might eventually flood Barr's valuable field, a dam that I was sorry to see busted up one day when I came back home.

Yet, as you can suppose, Vietnam has a way of never letting one go. One of the injured children I helped evacuate was a twelve-year-old boy from an orphanage on the South China Sea near Da Nang. Bùi Ngọc Hường. His father was a South Vietnamese soldier killed in the war. After his father's death, Hường was put in the orphanage by his mother, who ran off with another soldier. One day, while playing on the beach with other orphanage kids, he found something on the sand and touched it with his tongue. It was a "dragontooth" landmine. Made in America and dropped by our planes. It exploded. Hường's upper and lower lips and jaw were blown away. His hands were burned. When I found him back at his orphanage months later, he was dying of malnutrition, since he couldn't eat except through a straw. Nor could he be easily understood. The Vietnamese surgeon and head of the Da Nang regional hospital insisted we take him to the US for surgeries to repair his face and restore his ability to eat and talk. That was in 1969. By 1975, after numerous surgeries in Philadelphia, Hường was a tall, long-haired teenager who wanted to go home. He said he wanted to see his grandmother. He was sure she was still alive near Quang Ngai although he had no evidence for that. And we could find no relatives left in Vietnam, although we attempted a search through the Committee of Responsibility's Saigon office.

During Hường's many surgeries, he had stayed with friends of mine outside Philadelphia. But for the past two years he had been living with Lonnie and me in Warriors Mark. I found a job for him with Penn State's greenhouse keeper and gave the man a small amount of money to give to Hường each week as a salary for helping maintain the exquisite greenhouse plants, which must have reminded Hường of home . . . lush, leafy plants, bougainvillea, big banana trees. Hường liked the work and having money that he had earned himself and probably also the freedom of being on his own on campus and in the college town close by. The greenhouse director couldn't have been better with him.

On the evening when the war officially ended, April 30, 1975, we were all sitting in rocking chairs on the front porch of the farmhouse, Apples sleeping at our feet, Lonnie picking brambles off Apples's fur. I was smoking a cigar. Hường was quiet, watching mist gather in hollows down by the creek and thinking . . . who knows what. You may remember that church bells were rung all across the US that evening. To our amazement, someone had gone to the small country church on the hill across from us and was now ringing its bell across the valley.

I remember explaining to Hường why the bell was being rung, what it signified to Americans, not just in our little valley but everywhere across the US.

"Peace," I said. "Peace in Vietnam."

"Is it peace?" he said, with the bell's last toll. "Or only a bell ringing?"

———

Hường *did* go home. The Committee of Responsibility—that group of American doctors and volunteers that I worked for in Vietnam and who cared for Hường in the US—managed to contact Quaker volunteers working in Quang Ngai, who offered to help Hường when he returned. So, at eighteen, he flew back by himself to be met by COR workers in Saigon, who took him to our house on Hùynh Quang Tiên Street, where he stayed a week, taking in the heat and the crowded streets, hearing Vietnamese spoken everywhere, and talking with people in his native tongue. It must have been overwhelming and wonderful. After that week, when he seemed adjusted enough and ready to go, COR helped him manage his flights to Da Nang and Quang Ngai in provinces that were then peaceable but in the hands of the North Vietnamese army.

From Quang Ngai he wrote Lonnie and me a letter in quite good English. And, incredibly—after just a couple of days of hanging around the village market—he spotted his old grandmother. He was joyous. We were too.

Not long after that, we learned from the Quakers that Hường was shot and killed running away from a North Vietnamese roadblock. Apparently, he had panicked when his bus was stopped, and instead of staying put, he took off down the road. Perhaps he was afraid because of his stay in the US. The soldiers, we later heard, never really saw or spoke to him but only saw someone running away . . . tall, with long hair. Perhaps they thought he was an American.

Speak, Memory

I. THE BOOK AND THE LACQUERED BOX

So the soul, that drop, that ray
Of the clear fountain of eternal day,
Could it within the human flow'r be seen.

ANDREW MARVELL, "ON A DROP OF DEW"

The book's pages feel like cigar leaf;
its crackling spine flutters up a mildewed must.
Unlike the lacquered box which dry-warp detonated
—shattering pearled poet, moon, and willow pond—
the book survived to beg us both go back
to the Bibliothèque in the Musée at the Jardin in Saigon,
where I would lean from ledges of high windows
to see the zoo's pond, isled with Chinese pavilion,
arched bridge where kids fed popcorn to gulping carp,
and shaded benches, where whores fanned their makeup,
at ease because a man who feeds the peacocks
can't be that much of a beast. A boat ride,
a soda, a stroll through the flower beds.
On weekends the crowds could forget the war.

At night police tortured men in the bear pits,
one night a man held out the bag of his own guts,
which streamed and weighed in his open hands,
and offered them to a bear. Nearby, that night,
the moon was caught in willows by the pond,
shone scattered in droplets on the flat lotus pads,
each bead bright like the dew in Marvell's rose.

2. THE OPIUM PILLOW

A cool ceramic block, a brick
just larger than one's cheek,
cream-colored, bordered in blue,
a finely cracked glaze, but smooth,
a hollow bolster on which to lay
one's head before it disappears
in curls of acrid opium fumes
slowly turning in the tropical room
lit by a lampwick's resinous light
which flickers on the floor and throws
shadows snaking up a wall.
The man who serves us with his pipes,
with nicotined and practiced hands,
works a heated wad of rosin
"cooked the color of a cockroach wing"
into the pinprick of the fat pipe bowl.
He says, "Draw." One long draw
that pulls in combers of smoke rolling
down the lungs like the South China Sea,
crashing on the mind's frail shell
that rattles, then wallows and fills with sand.

I woke on wobbly legs to human cries.
Next door were Flynn and Stone
shouting and beating up an older man
they collared trying to steal their bikes.
Stone banged an M16 against the fellow's ear
then struck him in the stomach with its butt.
He doubled up and wheezed for air;
they slammed him out and down the stairs
and, red and sweating, walked back in.
I stammered "no" but much too late;

my words were lifting up like bubbles
rocking off the ocean's floor.
Ten days later, they were dead. Flynn
and Stone, who dealt in clarities of force,
who motorcycled out to report war,
shot down together. Dead on Highway One.
Some twenty years ago. Their only headrest
this pillow of dreams and calmest sleep
which once held echoes like a shell
now sits upon my study shelf
and ebbs out muffled echoes like a bell.

3. PRINCE BỬU HỘI'S WATCH

A long story. Of love and perfidy
ticking away in an old Omega
with a cracked crystal and a dusty face,
which the Prince's English friend gave me
just after his heart attack and early death.
We sat in her home in the Villa Ségur.
"It's awful having it here," she said.
Above the mantel from which she took the watch
was her photograph from years before
in sundress and shady hat, in Saigon,
with the Prince and Diem and Henry Cabot Lodge,
all cordial in their tropical white suits.
Lodge was smiling with tall, paternal grace
at the pudgy little man, earnest with goodwill,
whom we liked to call "the Churchill of Asia."
Diem would die the next day. Lodge already knew.
And Patricia and Prince Bửu Hội, Minister of Health
and nearly the fixer of a separate peace, would flee
with sympathies from the French ambassador.
One listens to the watch and sunlight shifts
as shadows shake through threshing palms,

through banyan and great sprays of bougainvillea.
The time that it keeps best is past.

4. THE PERFUME VIAL

Its smooth shape fits easily in the palm
as one takes it from the shelf to see
the little mandarin with outstretched arms,
cap, queue, and courtly gown.
One simple question strikes me as I look:
The doves that flutter just above his hands
—are they flying to or from them?

In Celebration of Spring

Our Asian war is over; others have begun.
Our elders, who tried to mortgage lies,
are disgraced, or dead, and already
the brokers are picking their pockets
for the keys and the credit cards.

In delta swamp in a united Vietnam,
a Marine with a bullfrog for a face
rots in equatorial heat. An eel
slides through the cage of his bared ribs.
At night, on the old battlefields, ghosts,
like patches of fog, lurk into villages
to maunder on doorsills of cratered homes,
while all across the USA
the wounded walk about and wonder where to go.

And today, in the simmer of lyric sunlight,
the chrysalis pulses in its mushy cocoon,
under the bark on a gnarled root of an elm.
In the brilliant creek, a minnow flashes
delirious with gnats. The turtle's heart
quickens its taps in the warm bank sludge.
As she chases a Frisbee spinning in sunlight,
a girl's breasts bounce full and strong;
a boy's stomach, as he turns, is flat and strong.

Swear by the locust, by dragonflies on ferns,
by the minnow's flash, the tremble of a breast,
by the new earth spongy under our feet:
that as we grow old, we will not grow evil,
that although our garden seeps with sewage,

and our elders think it's up for auction—swear
by this dazzle that does not wish to leave us—
that we will be keepers of a garden, nonetheless.

For the Missing in Action

Hazed with heat and harvest dust
the air swam with flying husks
as men whacked rice sheaves into bins
and all across the sunstruck fields
red flags hung from bamboo poles.
Beyond the last treeline on the horizon
beyond the coconut palms and eucalyptus
out in the moon zone puckered by bombs
(the dead earth where no one ventures)
the boys found it, foolish boys
riding buffaloes in craterlands
where at night bombs thump and ghosts howl.
Just a green patch on the raw earth.
And now they've led the farmers here,
the kerchiefed women in baggy pants,
the men with sickles and flails, children
herding ducks with switches—all
staring from a crater berm; silent.

In that dead place the weeds had formed a man
where someone died and fertilized the earth, with flesh
and blood, with tears, with longing for loved ones.
No scrap remained; not even a buckle
survived the monsoons, just a green creature,
a viny man, supine, with posies for eyes,
butterflies for buttons, a lily for a tongue.
Now when huddled asleep together
the farmers hear a rustling footfall
as the leaf-man rises and stumbles to them.

Mr. Giai's Poem

The French ships shelled Haiphong then took the port.
Mr. Giai was running down a road, mobilized
with two friends, looking for their unit in towns
where thatch and geese lay shattered on the roads
and smoke looped up from cratered yards. A swarm
of bullock carts and bicycles streamed against them
as trousered women strained with children, chickens,
charcoal, and rice toward Hanoi in the barrage lull.
Then, Giai said, they saw just stragglers.
Ahead, the horizon thumped with bombs.

At an empty inn they tried their luck
though the waiter said he'd nothing left.
"Just a coffee," said Mr. Giai. "A sip
of whiskey," said one friend. "A cigarette," the other.
Miraculously, these each appeared. Serene,
they sat a while, then went to fight.
Giai wrote a poem about that pause for *Ve Quoc Quan,*
the Army paper. Critics found the piece bourgeois.

Forty years of combat now behind him
—Japanese, Americans, and French.
Wounded twice, deployed in jungles for nine years,
his son just killed in Cambodia,
Giai tells this tale to three Americans
each young enough to be his son:
an ex-Marine once rocketed in Hué,
an Army grunt, mortared at Bong Son,
a C.O. hit by a stray of shrapnel,

all four now silent in the floating restaurant
rocking on moor-lines in the Saigon River.
Crabshells and beer bottles litter their table.
A rat runs a rafter overhead. A wave slaps by.
"That moment," Giai adds, "was a little like now."
They raise their glasses to the river's amber light,
all four as quiet as if carved in ivory.

South of LA

wet-suited surfers scud the green combers
and the freeway whines like a wire
here at San Onofre where reactor domes
hump up between sandcliffs and sea
and youngsters promenade the beach
in permed hair and sleekest tans
hoping like hell, for hell is just that:
not to be cast away, to be loved.

As egrets stalk the fouled lagoon
a coot clacks its beak in dry reeds
and, overhead, Camp Pendleton choppers,
Hueys and sleek Cobra gunships,
sweep dragonfly wings in churns of light.

I guess we know this all might blow,
that marsh and egrets, crabs and coots,
tanned teenagers and shimmering shoreline
could be no more than mulch and ash,
atomic smog just drifting out to sea,
drifting past the distant fogbank,
filtering down to the mid-Pacific ridge
that cooks up life in volcanic vents—that
someday our cells may chug through those shafts.

Hissarlik

Such is the will of Zeus, who has laid many
a proud city in the dust, as he will yet lay others.

HOMER, *THE ILIAD* 2.9.16–17

This is the dust
of nine cities,
royal as the poppy,

each grown
over the sediment
of the last.

Here the dust of Achaeans
and of Priam's sons
mingles

with the shards and stones,
the bones—remnants
of slaves and lords.

Nine cities,
born in turn
upon the death mounds

of the former,
entombing themselves,
building this hill.

This is the hill
of Hissarlik where
the limbs of countless

entwine and dissolve
under the common earth
which we sift and shovel

into fluted ash cans
that lie empty now
like broken white columns.

For Mrs. Cẩm, Whose Name Means "Brocaded Silk"

The ancients loved those poems with natural feel.
Hồ Chí Minh, "On Reading the *Anthology*
of a Thousand Poets"

In Vietnam, poets brushed on printed silk
those poems about clouds, mountains, and love.
But now their poems are cased in steel.

You lived beyond the Pass of Clouds
along the Perfume River, in Huế,
whose name means "lily."

The war has blown away your past.
No poem can call it back.
How does one start over?

You raise your kids in southern California;
run a key punch from 9:00 to 5:00,
and walk the beach each evening,

marveling at curls broken bare in crushed shells,
at the sheen and cracks of laved, salted wood,
at the pearling blues of rock-stuck mussels

all broken, all beautiful, accidents
which remind you of your life, lost friends
and pieces of poems that made you whole.

In tidal pools, the pipers wade
on twiggy legs, stabbing for starfish
with scissoring, poking, needle bills.

The wide Pacific flares in sunset.
Somewhere over there was once your home.
You study the things that start from scratch.

Nicely like a pearl is a poem
begun with an accidental speck
from the ocean of the actual.

A grain, a grit, which once admitted
irritates the mantle of thought
and coats itself in lacquers of the mind.

At 4:00 a.m., Asleep

I wanted to shoot the jerk
whining his wheels on an ice patch
dragging me from sleep
even before sparrows screech the dawn
up from snow-crusted choirs of forsythia
between houses somehow asleep.
But maybe the jerk is a her not a him
some poor drudge who's finally had it
after a long night of shouts and slaps.

Maybe this suburb isn't the dead zone.
Maybe others are awake . . . some old guy
sitting up with arthritis, chain-smoking,
or a mother, leaning over a crib
stroking her child crackling with phlegm,
or some man fishing in a toilet bowl
as his wife sobs into her hands and he spoons up
the blood clot, the embryo sac, to take to the doctor
to see what went wrong.

Thinking these things
before falling back to sleep, I realized
I was called out into a field of compassion
into a universe of billions of souls, and
that was a messenger now driving away.

For My Sister in Warminster General Hospital

The two birds augured something strange.
First, I saved the blackpoll warbler
that piped twice as the cat pounced
and clawed its slapping wings.
No blood. Alive, but the bird couldn't fly.
Just pecked my warm hands.
And slept the night in my fishing creel.
When I took it out the next morning
it peeped once before bounding to a hemlock,
cocked its head at me,
and then flew off to Argentina.

Then the junco sitting by the door.
I scooped it up, making my hands a nest.
When I let it loose later in the day
it bobbed away in those little arcs
that juncos make from bush to bush.
Two birds in the same day. Just exhausted.

I've heard of whole migrations blown off course,
looking for the Orkneys, lost in the Atlantic,
plummeting like hail onto a passing ship
where they flopped, faltered, and died.
All about, birds falling into swells.

So these auguries were for you, my sister,
asthmatic, gasping to flex your lungs
for ten days, or so I learned tonight.

When I was small and also could not breathe
you read me comics: Little Lulu and Scrooge McDuck

were our favorites. You read or made them up
while your skinny brother sat like a board in bed
and wheezed and panic widened in his eyes.

But I rested and then flew off.
Thirty years later, you force your lungs for air.
Consider: whole flocks lost and blown into the sea.
Consider the sailors looking from that deck,
while watching waves engulf the keening birds.
It makes no sense; it only happens.

You be the bird that fell down exhausted,
that rested and took off, a bit later in the day.

Anna Akhmatova Spends the Night on Miami Beach

Well, her book, anyway. The Kunitz volume
left lying on a bench, the pages
a bit puffy by morning, flushed with dew,
riffled by sea breeze, scratchy with sand
—the paperback with the 1930s photo
showing her in spangled caftan, its back cover
calling her "star of the St. Petersburg circle
of Pasternak, Mandelstam, and Blok,
surviving the Revolution and two World Wars."

So she'd been through worse ...
the months outside Lefortovo prison
waiting for a son who was already dead, watching
women stagger and reel with news of executions,
one mother asking, "Can you write about this?"
Akhmatova thought, then answered, "Yes."

If music lured her off the sandy bench
to the clubs where men were kissing
that wouldn't have bothered her much
nor the vamps sashaying in leather.
Decadence amid art deco fit nicely
with her black dress, chopped hair, Chanel cap.
What killed her was the talk, the empty eyes,
which made her long for the one person in ten thousand
who could say her name in Russian,
who could take her home, giving her a place
between Auden and Apollinaire
to whom she could describe her night's excursion
amid the loud hilarities, the trivial hungers
at the end of the American century.

Dipping a bucket into a well in which the
moon shines her silvery light
NGUYỄN KHẮC VIỆN, "NGUYEN DU AND KIEU,"
VIETNAMESE STUDIES

———————————

Passing through a Gate

One day, as the 1968 Tet fighting continued in and around Cần Thơ and the city was still under siege, two of my colleagues from International Voluntary Services—Hintze and Seraile—and I tried to drop off some food for our office manager, Phạm Văn Chánh, now holed up in a garage with some of his friends and afraid to leave in the mayhem of shooting that continued as ARVN troops, huddled behind an armored personnel carrier, fired into the nearby movie theater while Vietnamese Skyraiders strafed the university buildings behind our abandoned house a half mile away. We had planned a quick stop. Hintze, a farm boy from Idaho, was at the wheel. Seraile, who had just arrived in Vietnam after a stint in Ethiopia with the Peace Corps, said, "Make it quick."

Hintze kept the Land Rover running as I jumped out with a ham sandwich I had grabbed for Chánh at the besieged army mess hall just up the road. As I got a few steps away from the Rover, something hit me in the back and knocked me to my knees. I hadn't heard a thing. The guys in the Rover saw me fall down, then struggle up, bewildered, looking around. I remember Chánh and his friends waving at me from the open garage door. No one came out for me, but a stray mutt padded over and snatched the fallen sandwich. I staggered toward the garage. Reaching behind my shoulder, I was shocked to see blood. Later that day at an army outpost, I got X-rayed, probed, pumped with antibiotics, and bandaged up. Whatever hit me was left for later removal.

With the bombing of the university where I taught, I was finished with the International Voluntary Services. But legally, as a civilian conscientious objector, I still owed the US Selective Service another year of alternative service, so I had to come home to the US and apply for approval for another assignment.

Once back in Philadelphia, I contacted the Committee of Responsibility to Save War-Injured Children, a public charity begun by a group of doctors who volunteered their services at university hospitals across the US. COR needed a Vietnamese speaker to manage their Saigon office. Their board chairman was Dr. Herbert Needleman, who hired me as their new field representative and took me in. Literally. For my first few months back in the US, I lived with Dr. Needleman and his young family while I got my shrapnel wound treated at Temple University Hospital, where Needleman was on the psychiatric staff and where a COR doctor over in Surgery discovered that, besides my shrapnel wound, I had tubercular scarring on my lungs and amoebic dysentery in my gut. I weighed 115 pounds.

— —

In the fall of 1969, after I got better and after the Selective Service okayed my work for COR, I went back to Saigon to look after severely wounded children slated for treatment at teaching hospitals in the US. My job was to visit Vietnamese province hospitals, obtain referrals from Vietnamese or American doctors, talk to each child's parents for their approval, and then submit details of each case to a South Vietnamese Ministry of Health medical examining commission, establishing that any child we were proposing for US medical evacuation could not be treated adequately in Vietnam. My work in Saigon involved reams of legal paperwork for Saigon officials and a stream of telegrams back and forth to Dr. Needleman, each telegram requiring getting on a motorcycle and standing in line at the former French post office downtown. Fortunately, I had a capable colleague, Dick Berliner, also a former IVS teacher and a better speaker of Vietnamese than I was.

Sometimes, COR doctors would arrive from the US, each leaving their practices and families for a few weeks, to make the initial medical decisions. Berliner and I would guide them through South Vietnam hospitals and the bureaucracy in Saigon. Sometimes a Vietnamese surgeon or hospital director in the provinces would refer a child to us, and we would all travel to a hospital in the delta or up north. After the children were approved by a medical examining commission, Berliner and I would arrange for them to be flown from the provinces to Saigon and into the hands of the British surgical team working at Nhi Dong Children's Hospital, where the children were cared for while awaiting evacuation on a US Air Force hospital ship flying out of Tan Son Nhut Air Force Base. Instead of seats, the airplane had beds—and doctors and nurses. The children could go only on a space-available basis, first spaces going to wounded Americans. With each child we arranged for an English-speaking *convoyeuse* to go with them on the hospital plane and then on to their destinations in the United States, where the women would stay with them until the children were well enough to come home to their families.

Some of the children we brought to US hospitals were riddled with bullets, slashed by cluster bomb fléchettes, blinded and deafened by tossed grenades, had their lips and jaws shot away, their spines severed. Others had their limbs blown off, including one twelve-year-old boy left limbless except for one arm after a road-mine blast. Another boy had his chin glued to his chest by napalm. One girl had her eyelids burned off by a white phosphorus artillery shell that landed behind her house. One gunshot toddler survived the massacre of her family in a ditch because she was protected by their bodies, including her dead mother's.

I could go on. And, indeed, the memory of such suffering would have been my sole, unadulterated sense of Vietnam had not my job sometimes taken me into the countryside to reassure parents of what we could realistically do for their children at hospitals in the United States.

My visits to children's families in the countryside gave me a glimpse of another, more enduring Vietnam. Improbable as it may seem, these glimpses came on snatches of poetry and song that led me into a realm of beauty and wisdom beyond the mayhem of the war. And this is what I want to talk about in this essay: the poems sung by country people that drew me back to Vietnam not as the name of a war but as a culture of living and ancient poetry.

At first I had no clue about the cultural depth around me. I would be standing on a riverbank way out in the war zone as a little skiff motored by, and I would hear a bit of song float past me, sometimes without ever seeing the singer's face under the conical leaf hat from where her song drifted up to disappear in the stutter of the boat's two-cycle engine and the wave wash sloshing the muddy bank at my feet. Or I would be stuck at a Mekong ferry crossing waiting for a boat—waiting there with farmers returning home from markets. Sometimes by a river dock under big trees would be a blind singer with a twelve-string guitar entertaining and pan-handling. Back then I didn't have any idea what he was singing about.

Once I found myself way out in the delta north of Cần Thơ waiting in an orchard behind a family's house as they came to a decision about sending their thirteen-year-old son, his right arm shattered by artillery fire, to America in our care. COR had arranged surgery for him at University Hospital in Iowa. That day, off a dirt road, at their bamboo-thatched house under palm trees, I had come for their decision. While they conferred, I went out back to sit on a bench in their fruit orchard. Somewhere in the stands of bananas and papaya, a woman's voice started up in song. I was in my mid-twenties and in what you might call a heightened state because of what was happening inside and because being out in the countryside by myself was a risk. But the singing was lovely—just a lone voice drifting through the leaves. I couldn't see the woman but pictured her picking bananas or snagging papaya into one of those little wire baskets at the end of a long pole. Inside the simple house, a momentous decision was being made about the boy whose left upper arm had been severed by shrapnel but was now held together by a plaster-of-paris cast and fed by an underarm sliver of flesh that carried the critical arteries and nerves. He could still move his fingers, so there was hope. At the Cần Thơ hospital weeks earlier, the family had refused the surgeon's advice to have their son's arm removed. Now the exposed splintered bone tips were starting to decay.

After what seemed like forever, they came out with some tea and a sliced mango. It was late in the afternoon, and everyone knew I had to get out of there before too long. Yes, they would send their son for surgery in America. They made me promise to bring him back when it was all over.

All during our talk, drifting in the background of this charged moment, oblivious to the drama in the home and yet calling from some other realm, was the woman's song.

———

Nearly a year and a half later, after the boy indeed had his arm saved and was returned to his family, my two years of alternative service to the military officially ended. I was back again in the US. Through the support of my old teachers at Penn State, I got a job as an instructor teaching freshman comp and introductory linguistics. A year later, I got married. Settled as I seemed to be, I was nonetheless stalked by agitations, as almost every moment of my academic routine was invaded by memories of the war and of the friends I had left in Vietnam. It was hard to sit still, to read, to grade papers, or even to attend receptions or cocktail parties with colleagues my age who had gone from college to graduate school and to the classroom without a hitch. I had recently broken my left foot in a faculty–grad student baseball game and was going nuts sitting on the porch of the farmhouse I rented with my wife, my foot propped up in a cast, my head swarming with memories, and drinking too much.

My agitation was so intense that at the start of the summer break I persuaded my wife to drop me off, with my backpack and crutches, on Interstate 80, which ran just north of us from New York all the way to San Francisco. That month, I hitchhiked from Pennsylvania to California and back to see a Saigon friend now hospitalized in San Francisco. My plan was to use a CB walkie-talkie to get rides. In the event of trouble, I carried in my backpack a letter from my research dean, Thomas Magner, which said I was on a research project and asked that I be "afforded any courtesies." It may have saved me from arrest when a state trooper stopped me just outside the twin tunnels on Route 80 in Wyoming, read my letter, looked amused, said, "OK, Professor, get in," and dropped me off at the next rest stop.

Back home at Penn State that fall, I got a letter from Crystal Eastin, a friend working in Saigon at Dispatch News, which broke the My Lai story. With her letter were some "folk" poems that she asked me to translate. A Vietnamese guy working in the news office had told her that these were *ca dao*,[1] poems sung for hundreds of years, and that if you wanted to know anything about the Vietnamese, this was the place to start. *So,* I thought, *that* is what I heard when I was traveling into the countryside for COR: moments of poetry in a living oral tradition . . . the woman in the boat, the blind singer at the river crossing. When I started to translate Crystal's bunch of poems, my agitation both increased and was directed. I began to understand how these poems might represent a culture Americans knew nothing about even as they were destroying it. I made plans to return and collect those sung poems on tape. I applied to the National Endowment for the Humanities and received a Younger Humanist grant.

So in 1971, with the war staggering on, along with my wife (she just out of college! What were we thinking?), I was back in Vietnam, where she would teach English to Saigon University students while I would spend the next year traveling the Vietnamese countryside collecting *ca dao*. My plan was simple: I would walk up to farmers and fishermen, and girls minding their little brothers and sisters, or women working old Singer pedal sewing machines in their stilt houses above the Mekong, and I would ask them to sing their favorite poems into my tape recorder. Naive, I know, but somehow it worked.

Out in the country and war zone, I must have seemed very peculiar but not exactly threatening: a lone, long-haired American, not wearing a uniform, carrying only a green Harvard book bag and a Sony tape recorder. I am still amazed that these country people even talked to me, much less agreed to sing poetry into my recorder. In that whole year of recording, I never encountered anyone who did not know some *ca dao*. It was everywhere, it was like "dipping a bucket into a well" as the scholar Nguyễn Khắc Viện wrote, "in which the moon shines her silvery light." I recorded some five hundred poems that year from about thirty-five singers from the Mekong Delta, the Central Highlands, and the old capital of Huế. *Đi một ngày đàng, học một sàng khôn.* "Go out one day," the proverb says, "and come back with a basket full of wisdom."

So, while my wife was back in Saigon instructing her soldier-students on the English past tense and telling them not to bring their M16s into the classroom but to stack them on the porch outside, I was heading off on forays into the Mekong Delta to collect sung folk poetry, leaving Saigon for dusty country roads swept for landmines each morning, traveling on buses filled with farmers headed home with their bamboo baskets of live chickens. From the bus terminal in My Tho, I would take a cab or cyclo to the big Mekong ferry, which would take me to the other side of the river to board a smaller boat to Cồn Phụng, Phoenix Island, a mid-river religious sanctuary belonging to the followers of the Venerable Nguyễn Thành Nam—better known as Ông Đạo Dừa, "The Coconut Monk."

Phoenix Island seemed a best bet for starting my project. It was relatively safe. Until then in the course of the war, neither the US, the Viet Cong, or the Saigon army had blasted the place. And because it wasn't safe for me to travel *anywhere* alone, and because the followers at Phoenix Island came from all over the Delta, I figured their varied regional backgrounds and dialects could bring to my recorder a variety of styles in the oral tradition. Like the echo of the island's huge temple bell—struck day and night by a heavy mallet swung from a gantry rope by two monks—the Coconut Monk's followers carried all the Mekong Delta's riverine culture in their poems—poems in which one hears of the lone fish swimming off without a trace, of churning waters rattling the glass lamps of the fish traps, of a river rising to separate two lovers, of ducks paddling at evening and egrets flying in, and of the owl, like the Coconut Monk in his solitary meditation perch, which "nests only at the tip of the island."

One morning, Đạo Lê Văn Phúc, a young monk with a wispy beard, my friend and mentor, took me to meet a woman who, although she had never gone to school or learned to read or write, could recite perfectly metrical verse that she composed in a trance. A catwalk plank led from the shaded path to her house raised on pylons over the river, where she lived in two small rooms of bamboo and thatch. As we approached, she stood at her door. She was unusually tall. Her long black hair was shot with gray and tied in a bun; her rough hands and weathered face were unusually large. She stared at me with close-set eyes. I had the feeling, as we were introduced, that her mouth was ready to break into a grin, perhaps at the incongruity of our meeting or perhaps in the way crazy people sometimes do because, I suppose, they find it infinitely amusing when they meet yet another self-serious creature, this one an American.

A pungent, complex aroma drifted from her tiny house with the river air. Inside the door, I could see bundles of herbs hanging from the rafters. Sister Liên-Hương (Lotus Essence) sold herbs for a living.

I set up my tape recorder. With the three of us still standing in front of her door, she started to sing her poems in a high, cracked voice:

Clear Skies, Clear Sea

Others plant for profit.
I just go out and watch everything:

rilling water, sky, slow clouds,
wind and rain, day, dark night.
Lying on a cozy rock, watching
clear skies, still sea, calm heart.

Người ta đi cấy lấy công,
Tôi đây đi cấy còn trông nhiều bề.
Trông trời, trông nước, trông mây,
Trông mưa, trong gió, trông ngày, trông đêm.
Trông cho chân cứng đá mềm,
Trời trong, bể lặng mới yên tấm lòng.

When she finished, I asked her how she learned to sing. She said she
started singing when she was about twenty-seven and living in a Cao Dai
nunnery in Tay Ninh, northwest of Saigon.

"What preceded your first poem?" I asked.

She looked at me, perplexed, a little shocked.

Perhaps, I thought, my Vietnamese wasn't clear.

When Phúc rephrased my question, she looked at me nervously. And
then, after a pause, she mumbled to Phúc something I couldn't follow but
which seemed to embarrass him.

Phúc turned to me and said, "She says she was in a period for several
years . . . of insanity. When she got the power to sing about Buddha, her
mind cleared."

When she was about eleven, she told us, she was paralyzed on one side.
A famous wandering monk, Ông Sư Bán Khoai—"The Monk Who Sells
Potatoes"—came along and her parents asked him to cure her. They were
not rich, but they promised him anything of theirs that he wanted. He
picked a leaf from a pear tree and gave it to her. Her paralysis disappeared.
Her parents asked him what he wanted. He said he wanted her. After that
she followed him around for about two years until, after her first menstru-
ation, he left her at the nunnery in Tay Ninh. She never saw or heard from
him again.

When she was with him, she said, he could make himself look like a mad
fool, or a leper, or a blind beggar. In the guise of a blind beggar, he often

set up by the roadside a little grill on which he roasted potatoes. Peasants, seeing that he was blind, would sometimes steal from him. When they did, he would launch into a sermon in *sấm giảng* oracular verse about the realms of Hell, startling the peasants and causing them to consider their ways.

During those months, as I walked about under the tenuous protections of the Coconut Monk with my friend Đạo Phúc, I heard a lot about monks who used to roam the countryside with inspired missions and wonderful names. Ever since Buddhism began making its way east from India through Indochina in the centuries before the Christian era, there must have been local men and women, filled with doctrine and pieces of doctrine, wandering about the countryside preaching. The Monk Who Sells Potatoes (Ông Sư Bán Khoai). The Monk of the Western Peace (Đức Phật Thầy Tây-An). And the Coconut Monk, Nguyễn Thành Nam, who once studied agriculture in Paris and was now sitting in his perch at the tip of the island, teaching with symbols, with political theater, and without any words.

—— · ——

One morning just at dawn, Phúc and I were crossing the river on a big, two-deck wooden boat from Phoenix Island. About fifty island people were going to sell their fish and farm produce at the My Tho market. Mists were swirling off the river. Egrets, flapping away on great wings, fled before our noisy engine, an ancient John Deere tractor engine that a French plantation owner must have imported in the thirties. Around mid-river, a US Riverine Patrol cutter began to overtake us, bleating its huge horn. For some reason, our captain did not cut the engine when the gunboat flashed its signal and horn. So the cutter started firing a deck gun across our bow, the bullets skipping in the waves about twenty feet in front of us. Everybody on deck started shouting at the captain down in the noisy engine room where he hadn't heard anything. We stopped and drifted as the cutter came up alongside, cannons trained on us, its deck bristling with American sailors waving guns and shouting gibberish Vietnamese and pidgin English.

The first of them to board us, a .45 pistol in hand, stopped dead for a moment when he saw me sitting in the back with Phúc, who was going to My Tho to have his fortune read by a specialist. The sailor elbowed another sailor holding an M16, who took note, and then they went about their business questioning bewildered farmers, all of us just sitting very still as the two boats rocked together and the sailors looked into knapsacks and bundles, demanding IDs. As this went on, the two sailors came back and asked for mine.

"Be polite, Mr. John," Phúc advised.

Without saying anything I handed them my ID. My National Endowment grant allowed me an ID card issued by the US embassy in Saigon. On it was printed that "if captured" I should "be afforded the rank of major in the US Army."

As the sailor handed it back he took in my long hair and drawstring monk's pants. I could see myself in his mind's eye, changing now from a rumored Russian adviser to a deep-cover CIA agent. He said, "You know, we were up river one day in VC country and we went down this narrow inlet and found this hootch where there wasn't supposed to be any dwellings. So we sneaked up on it and you know what we found?"

I shook my head in wonder.

"These two long-hairs. Hippies. Vietnamese hippies. I mean, they were sitting at a table drinking tea out in this free-fire zone—nothing but crickets, craters, and VC—and they were just kind of laughing and talking. It blew my mind. I mean, they weren't VC or nothing. They didn't even run when they saw us, just started laughing again. They looked kind of high. I felt bad, but we had to take them in as draft-dodgers."

— • —

Like dragons, the great rivers of Vietnam—the Red and the Black in the north, the Perfume in the center, and the Mekong in the south—give nurture and good fortune, for it is along the alluvial plains of their many tributaries that the Vietnamese have prospered over the long centuries in an agricultural civilization that may date as far back as the Đông Sơn culture of 2000 BCE. In the West, we often measure and mark civilizations by their physical monuments: cathedrals, castles, ramparts. In Vietnam, swept by annual monsoons, agrarian dynasties with a cultural continuity of millennia have left few monuments more enduring than the oral poetry and song known today as *ca dao.*

Ca dao are always lyrical, sung to melodies without instrumental accompaniment by an individual singing in the first person, not the narrative, storytelling third person of ancient oral poetry in the West. The range of *ca dao* includes children's game songs, love songs, lullabies, riddles, work songs, and reveries about spiritual and social orders. No stories are plotted. The singer, to quote Confucius, merely "gives vent to his complaint." Usually the poems are quite brief. Lyrics complete in one couplet are common, usually based on a fourteen-syllable construct shorter even than the Japanese haiku. But the form also invites a stringing together of such couplets linked by internal rhyme, as in *ca dao*'s greatest *written* manifestation: the 3,250 lines of Nguyễn Du's classic, *Truyện Kiều, The Tale of Kiều.*

The poets of *ca dao* come from the rural population of Vietnam, which, as ever, represents almost 90 percent of the total population, and it is here that *ca dao* still prospered in 1971 and prospers now. Indeed, the conditions for nurturing *ca dao* lyrics are not the din and rush of the city or the entertainments of radio or television, or even the power of literacy. *Ca dao* prospers among people who do not have easy access to writing or electronic media. It prospers in villages where the lone singer can hear his or her voice against the drone of crickets, the slap of water, or the rustling of banana leaves in the wind. *Ca dao* are part of the realm of country life. In my ventures decades ago, I recorded children and adults during the day when they took breaks from farming or boatbuilding. At night, by kerosene lamp, typically I would start taping with one person and then perhaps eight or so neighbors would gather, joke about my microphone, sit down with us on the floor, and urge another to begin singing. The lyrics that one person sang would remind him of more and, as others were reminded of poems they knew, the singing would shift from one person to another until it was time for bed. Sometimes the war intruded as firefights would start up across the river, but the singing continued on our island, where a few times I recorded to the occasional whomp of mortar or rifle fire.

In nine months, I recorded about thirty-five singers—men, women, and children—who gave me about five hundred lyrics. (Approximately five thousand *ca dao* are thought to be alive at any given time.) The youngest was a boy of five; the oldest, a woman well into her seventies. While the age range was considerable (with enough youngsters to indicate that the tradition was still being carried on), most of my recordings came from a half-dozen men with wide repertoires of several hundred poems each. In age and occupation, the men included a nineteen-year-old farmer-monk from the Mekong Delta and a seventy-year-old former palanquin bearer for a mandarin of the last imperial court in Huế. From these singers, I gathered love laments, songs about birds and beasts, poems of social protest and social order (usually renegotiating Confucian obligations), patriotic and political poems, lullabies, courting songs with male and female replies, and children's game songs. I succeeded best when I had the help of someone who knew the dialect and the singers. Without local help, I could not have completed the recordings. People like Đạo Phúc on Phoenix Island, or Mrs. Cẩm up in Huế, were locally trusted, knew the local dialect, and would correct my transcriptions, almost all of which had never been written down in Vietnamese before.

— • —

What structures of language and rules of poetry are at work in this oral, unwritten tradition? And how does a translator deal with them?

Vietnamese, similar in some respects to Chinese, belongs to the Mon-Khmer language family of the Austro-Asiatic phylum.[2] Depending on the dialect, five or six pitches or tones can apply to any syllable to render its specific meaning and sound. In writing, these tones are indicated by diacritical marks in the *quốc-ngữ* roman alphabet, the modern "national script." Every syllable in the language carries one of these tones, each establishing the meaning of the syllable. (Most words in Vietnamese are monosyllables.) For example, the form /*la*/ can hold six separate meanings depending on the tone employed:

la: to shout (high-level tone)
là: to be (falling tone)
lả: tired (falling-rising tone)
lã: insipid (high-constricted, broken tone)

lá: leaf (high-rising tone)

lạ: strange (low-constricted tone)

In the basic couplet form below, called a *lục-bát* (or "six-eight"), an eight-syllable line follows a six-syllable line and is linked to it by rhyme and word tone:

Hỡi	*cô*	*tát*	*nước*	*bên*	*đàng.*	
Oh,	girl	bailing	water	by	roadside,	

Sao	*cô*	*múc*	*ánh*	*trăng*	*vàng*	*đổ đi?*
Why	(girl)	ladle	light	moon	gold	pour out?

(Oh, girl, bailing water by the roadside,
why pour off the moon's golden light?)

When the poems are sung, syllables may be added or dropped, often for vocal ornamentation, but all *ca dao* observe rules of meter and rhyme.[3] And while tones fall at random in speech or in prose, in poetry the tones are regulated to fall at certain feet in the prosodic line. The second, sixth, and eighth syllables of each line must be "even" tones (like *la* or *là,* in the above), whereas the fourth syllables must be any one of the other tones, which are all considered "sharp."

Rhymes properly fall only on words that have "even" tones. In the couplet above, the sixth and final syllable of the first line (*đàng*) rhymes with the sixth syllable of the next line (*vàng*). The eighth syllable of the second line (*đi*) is a potential new rhyme that the singer could use to start linking in any number of additional couplets, folding in new rhymes each time. All this is retained in the oral poet's ear. While it might seem a complex construct for poets who do not read or write, the six-eight couplet is only one of several prosodic forms available to them, although it is the most commonly employed.

Adding to this musical richness are the melodies, from which the poems are complexly inseparable. In playing my tapes for the renowned musicologist Professor Trần Văn Khê of the National Center for Scientific

Research in Paris, I learned that *ca dao* are sung to ditonic, tritonic, tetra-tonic, and pentatonic scales, with the latter scale the most frequent. Furthermore, according to Professor Khê, the melodies themselves are embellishments or extensions of the word-pitch patterns set up by the word choices. Often the melodies are unfixed, "singing without song," or cantillations, a term applied to the early religious music of the West.[4] It is this wedding of music to meter that is the main mnemonic device that carries these poems across the centuries on the voices of people who rarely write them down.

My standard question—How did you learn the poem?—usually seemed a bit odd to the singers. (Although, at the same time, my interest in *ca dao* never seemed strange to them since poetry is central to rural culture.) When pressed on how they learned a poem, singers would pause and say something like, "Oh, I heard it from my mother who sang it around the house"—around the house, as routine as the chickens, the sound of wind in the palms, or the voices of relatives. Of the thirty-five individu-als I recorded that year, only one told me he often composed his poems himself. Everyone else—except perhaps for Sister Liên-Hương—was just passing a poem along. No one claimed to have set out to "learn" a poem.

Where did all this singing start? How old is the *ca dao* tradition? Clues from individual poems, hidden in lines such as "In the Year of the Dragon, God sent down a flood" (1904), or those holding a reference to the "coins of Vạn-Lịch" (minted 1573–1620), reveal only that the poems could not have been composed *before* those dates. More revealing are clues from the word-stock of *ca dao*, which indicates few Chinese borrowings, suggesting a native origin for the folk poetry, unlike Vietnamese *literary* poetry with its strong Chinese influences. Indeed, modern scholars generally agree that *ca dao* represent a native tradition.[5]

But how long have Vietnamese been composing *ca dao*?

In an attempt to date the *ca dao* tradition, in 1972 I made a trip into central Vietnam to record Mường singers near Ban Mê Thuột. After the signing of the 1954 Geneva Accords, the entire village left the North and settled in the South, in the Highlands. Linguists say that the Mường and

Vietnamese languages are 67 percent cognate, indicating through lexico-statistic dating a common language until about one thousand years ago. I wanted to see whether the various prosodic structures and singing habits of Vietnamese *ca dao* existed as well among the Mường, a population generally described as more archaic in their cultural habits than the Vietnamese. The Mường—making a separation between their upland selves and the lowland Vietnamese—call Vietnamese *mọl chợ,* "the market people."[6] Indeed, in my Mường recordings and in the transcriptions made by Milton Barker of the Summer Institute of Linguistics, one can find all the traditional Vietnamese forms of *ca dao* (such as the six-eight, double seven, and seven-seven: six-eight meters), suggesting a common origin, perhaps one that evolved from a Mon-Khmer singing tradition as old as the 4,000-year-old Đông Sơn culture and the ancient origins of the Vietnamese before the Mường and Vietnamese separated into highland and lowland cultures. So looking at the parallel singing tradition of the Mường ethnic group suggests that Vietnamese have been singing *ca dao* for more than a thousand years and probably much longer.[7]

The uses of *ca dao* extend well beyond the countryside. The oral poetry has always fed the written literature, as it does today in the literary fiction and poetry of postwar Vietnam. Even ordinary people with public school educations often choose the forms of *ca dao* when they want to write poetry. During the war, for example, North Vietnamese soldiers sent *ca dao* to each other and to their families at home, writing them down in their government-issue notebooks, crammed with copies of letters home, with medical records, with commendations, and with technical instructions for things such as how to figure a mortar's trajectory. These notebooks were taken from them when the soldiers were captured or killed and then photographed in Saigon for whatever military intelligence they might contain. A huge trove of these notebooks was collected by the Combined Document Exploitation Center on Tân Sơn Nhứt Air Force Base and now, declassified, can be read on microfilm. Here is a poem written in *ca dao* meter by Lê Ngọc Hiệp, who fought for eighteen years with the Ninth Battalion of the 101st NVA Regiment. He died near Tây Ninh in South Vietnam in March 1970. In his notebook, along with a picture of his wife, was a poem he had written to a fellow soldier and childhood friend. When he thinks of their returning in peace to their home village, he thinks of hearing *ca dao:*

When I got back to base
I sensed something had happened.
They said you went to hospital
And my heart was torn and sad.
I always think of you, Bùi Hữu Phái.
Your life runs out like a red silk banner.
Your many friends are waiting
Anxious for news about you.
Dear brother, my feelings well up
And I wish so much to see you.
Stronger than oceans or mountains,
Because mountains fall and seas dry up,
My feelings for you endure.
My feelings for you, unshakable.
You and I must keep safe
And march home in victory soon.
I came to Hà Tây on the first ship
Nurturing this dream, not losing heart.
Perhaps we mustn't dream about life.
Life is now too hard, dear brother.
So many dreams float in the air.
The more I think, the sadder I get.
How can one find his way to the future?
I think of you and weep these long nights.
I think of us chatting in an immense dusk,
Listening to poems sung in the evening,
The two of us drinking tea together.
Wouldn't that be a happy moment?
These images seem so real in this poem,
But right now they're hard to believe.
As I hold this pen and write you.

Translating *ca dao,* to quote again the late literary and cultural critic Nguyễn Khắc Viện, "is like drawing a bucket of water from a well where the moon is mirrored and unavoidably losing the silvery shine of her light." How can a translator capture that light? No translator can convey the sung musical melodies or the patterns of word tone so essential to the poems. Word tone is not phonemic to English. One can only hope, through the play of rhyme and meter and imagery, to give some inkling of this vast, ongoing tradition.

On December 24, 1971, in the old city of Huế, I was invited to meet eighty-year-old Lê Thanh Cảnh, a former mandarin in the last imperial court, unusually tall, whiskered, with a raspy voice and a mischievous twinkle. Decades earlier, in the "change of season" of the revolution, he had bicycled some three hundred miles from Huế to Hanoi to join the Viet Minh government, but discovering that he didn't like it very much, he bicycled back to Huế.

Still energetic in his old age, he was a collector of *ca dao* and showed me his notebooks where he had transcribed poetry from the region. This was unusual because while everyone seemed to know the oral poetry, it was usually just taken for granted. Few modern scholars or retired mandarins like Mr. Cảnh actually studied it, favoring instead the complex literary tradition of Chinese influence. Mr. Cảnh was delighted that someone was actually going to record *ca dao,* and, along with Mrs. Cẩm from the American Library, he took me to meet two men, Phan Văn Kha, fifty-four, a river merchant on the Perfume River, and Trần Ngọc Hảo, a seventy-year-old with a trailing white beard who had been one of Mr. Cảnh's palanquin bearers. With the five of us sitting on a shady veranda near a tributary of the Perfume River, Mr. Hảo sang the poem below, breaking the meter and rhyme to bend and embellish the notes.[8]

Evening, and all around the King's Pavilion
people are sitting, fishing, sad and grieving,
loving, in love, remembering, waiting, watching.
Whose boat plies the river mists

offering so many river songs
to move these mountains and rivers, our nation?

Trước bến Phu Văn Lâu
Chiều chiều trước bến Phu Văn Lâu.
Ai ngồi, ai câu, ai rầu, ai thảm,
Ai thương, ai cảm, ai nhớ, ai đợi, ai trông.
Thuyền ai thấp thoáng bến sông,
Đưa chi nhiều câu mái đẩy,
Chạnh lòng nước non.

When Mr. Hảo got to the last line, to keep him from wandering off
from the closure of the meter, Mr. Cảnh smacked the smooth plank floor
with his palm and for a moment all we heard was river water, a bird twit-
tering, muffled voices from the distant market, and the tolling bell of the
Linh Mụ Pagoda. For a moment, we were all speechless. It was as if a door
had opened to a vanished world, where we had lingered a bit, and now we
were back in our own world, although still in Huế, the old imperial capital
with its thousands of deaths and its near destruction a few years earlier
during the Tet Offensive of 1968. In just a few more months, during the
spring offensive of 1972, it would nearly fall to North Vietnamese troops
and tanks.

The "King's Pavilion," called Phu Văn Lâu,[9] was the poem-writing
place on the Perfume River where the Vietnamese kings, now subjects
of the French, could sit with their courtiers and friends, drink, watch the
moon, compose poems, and even gamble on poetry contests. The king
alluded to in the poem is the teenage "Emperor" Duy Tân, who reigned
from 1907 to 1916. Duy Tân was installed as king at the age of eight by
the French colonial authorities, perhaps because they thought a child
might be more manageable than his rebellious predecessors, Hàm Nghi
(r. 1884–1885) and Duy Tân's father, Thành Thái (r. 1889–1907), who
were both sent into exile, the former to Algeria, and the latter to Réunion
Island, a French département d'outre-mer, 422 miles east of Madagascar in
the Indian Ocean. But the child king grew up. Like his father, Duy Tân
became an "outlaw king," running off to the jungle with his royal court

until tracked down by the Sûreté and exiled, like his father, to Réunion. He was finally allowed to return to Vietnam but died in a plane crash on his way back in 1945.

Mr. Cảnh wanted me to know that there was something special about this *ca dao*. It held a secret. It had been *written,* not composed orally, by a royal relative of Duy Tân, Prince Ưng Bình, who had it slipped into the oral tradition. Hidden in the poem was a couplet ("Whose boat plies the river mists / offering so many river songs") from the famous *Tale of Kiều,* the Vietnamese classic that even unlettered peasants often know by heart. It was therefore a political poem, attempting to stir popular sentiment for the king who had gone into hiding in 1916 while the people in Huế, and indeed the nation, were hoping for his successful escape from the French.

— ▸ ◂ —

Years passed before I encountered the poem again . . . in Bulgaria. In the meantime I had become an academic, published a novel and some books of poetry and translation, and had pretty much forgotten how to speak Vietnamese.

I had been invited to a meeting of writers in Sofia, Bulgaria, during the height of the Cold War in the mid-1980s, as the US was threatening to move its nuclear weapons farther east in Europe, and the Soviets were threatening to move theirs west into Poland. The American guests included the distinguished poets Denise Levertov, Maxine Kumin, and William Meredith, as well as fiction writers Erskine Caldwell and William Gaddis. I never figured out how we were chosen to be invited. Probably many others had been invited but had declined the visit, as had John Updike, famous in Bulgaria for his own Vietnam-era visit there, resulting in his *Bech: A Book* and some political trouble for the renowned poet Blaga Dimitrova.

Along with the Americans were writers from everywhere on the planet. The Bulgarian Writers' Union put up about four hundred of us at their government's expense at the Hotel Parc Moskva. It must have cost a fortune to feed this literary battalion, provide us with plane tickets and city tours and give each of us a packet of spending money with about one hundred dollars in *leva*.

My visit to Bulgaria was the first time I encountered *North* Vietnamese.

The US and Vietnam still had no diplomatic relations. Indeed, the US had levied a trade embargo against the impoverished nation. I was curious about them and had given one of their delegation poets a copy of my first book of *ca dao* translations. That made them curious. How come this American spoke Vietnamese in the *southern* dialect? Where did he learn it? Why?

One afternoon I came back to the hotel to find about eight of the Vietnamese delegation sitting in the main lobby. They called me over. It had been fourteen years since I had any reason to speak Vietnamese and I was embarrassed. I could hardly understand them, much less reply. "That's okay," one said in French. "Sit down. Do you know French?"

I knew a little French. So they began again asking me in French about what I had done in Vietnam. Soon it was rapid-fire questioning from several people at once and it was bewildering. I flushed when I first realized I was being *interrogated,* albeit in the hotel lobby where other poets were talking nearby or walking to the elevators or to the bar. . . . Yevtushenko with his entourage of pretty women . . . various Party hacks from Bloc and Third World countries . . . no-name writers happy for the free trip. When I tried to explain my conscientious objection to the military (which one would assume was a nearly unknown concept in Vietnam for anyone not a Buddhist monk), it seemed I just couldn't make myself clear enough. My answers weren't complete, weren't satisfying. I was beginning to feel very uncomfortable but realized if I got up to go, it would just confirm their apparent suspicions that I was a CIA agent sent to spy on them. Now they were slipping some English into the flow of Vietnamese and French.

Finally, the guy who seemed to be in charge raised a hand for the others to stop. In his other hand he had the first edition of *Ca Dao Việt Nam* that I had given one of his colleagues. He began to flip through the poems and translations. We all went silent. Then he stopped on the last poem in the book, the poem above about King Duy Tân.

"Who wrote this poem, Professor Balaban?" he asked and smiled.

I smiled back. I could see where this was going. He had said *wrote.* Either he did not know anything about the folk poetry, or he did and was laying a trap for me. Either way I knew my way out and laid a little trap of my own.

"As you know," I said, "*ca dao* are not written. They are oral, passed down by song."

His smile faded. He looked at his compatriots who were *really* quite quiet. *This American is a spy.*

"... but *this* one," I added, "is unusual. It has a line in it from the *The Tale of Kiều* and refers to the disappearance of young King Duy Tân..."

"Yes, yes," he said, with some excitement, "who *wrote* it?"

"Ưng Bình. Whose pen name," I added, "was Thúc Giạ Thị."

Now everyone was smiling. *This American is okay.* Only a real translator could absorb a detail like that. I had been vetted through poetry.

Vetted through poetry. What a concept for the spymasters at Langley. Nonetheless, traditionally in Vietnam, skill in poetry is emblematic of an especially bright, honed mind and leadership. Even the "Marxist mandarins" who led the war against the US had studied poetry in Chinese and Vietnamese. Hồ Chí Minh could write classically metered poetry in both languages. If my interrogator was from Huế, as his knowledge of Prince Ưng Bình would indicate, he would have seen, carved in jade on a panel at the Long An Palace, the famous poetic palindrome, written by Emperor Thiệu-Trị (r. 1841–1847) for his "intellectual recreation," extensively described by Pierre Daudin, the French mathematician.[10] In the ideograms of this sun-shaped poem—the sun being the emblem of heavenly mandate—are twelve perfectly rhyming, seven-syllable, eight-line poems, with each new sunray or character being the start of a new poem, whether one reads from the outside in, or the inside out; left to right, or right to left.

Also, as a Marxist functionary trained in Hanoi, my interrogator in Sofia might very well have also seen the memorial stelae for doctoral candidates at the Temple of Literature. They, too, were carved in stone and are still there. One from the medieval period speaks to the need for vitality and precision in language. To be sure, such maxims on the interconnection between verbal precision and national vitality—and, of course, the poetry that flowed from such idealistic notions—will not bring back 58,219 dead Americans or over 4,000,000 Vietnamese, north and south, military and civilian, who perished in our then-longest war. Nor can such literary notions repair damage done to individuals and societies surviving the war. But perhaps they provide clues to what went wrong, both in that war and others since, where the speeches of politicians are once again routinely imprecise, befogged, clumsy, inaccurate, and lying, *perhaps not even deliberately* because that is an abiding predicament for those who speak without care or precision and, if that person is a national leader, an elected official, woe to the nation.

The East Asian value placed on poetry, the most skilled verbal art, was apparently still part of the intellectual equipment of a Communist Party functionary at the Hotel Parc Moskva in Bulgaria in 1985.

— • —

The last time I encountered the Duy Tân poem was in 2006, in Huế, at an international conference on Nôm ancient script writing, cosponsored by the foundation I started in 1999 with two Vietnamese colleagues. My wife and I were there with our twenty-one-year-old daughter. We hadn't been there since 1972 when my wife and I, with all other Americans, had to flee the city that was about to fall to North Vietnamese troops. (But it did not, partly because of a ferocious air and artillery bombardment, but mainly because the North Vietnamese tank units were moving so fast they simply ran out of gas.)

Now, thirty-four years later, across the river from our hotel was the famous Citadel and its royal palaces, with their moats and walled compounds, exquisite bonsai and topiary, water gardens, and massive gates. Before them, on the riverbank, under the shade of huge tamarind trees, was Phu Văn Lâu, the royal moon-watching and poetry pavilion of the poem. We took a cab to see it.

What once was a handsome wooden pavilion was now repaired with concrete supports but still preserving some of its original, delicate roof carpentry. As with all royal buildings, up on the ridge of the roof, two guardian dragons coiled on the tiles where ceramic flames leapt up from a round mirror, the emblem for "the face of Heaven." Where kings and courtiers had sat for centuries before, drinking wine and matching wits in poetry, a young couple was smooching on the steps facing the river.

All around the pavilion, the scene was very much the same as it was in the Ưng Bình poem of a hundred years before, with people sitting about catching the breeze off the river under the shade of big trees. Three elderly white-haired couples were enjoying a picnic on the grass. When they noticed us, one of the retirees struggled to his feet to say, *"Bonjour, mes amis."*

"Bonjour, Monsieur," my wife and I said together in singsong politesse, as our daughter looked quizzically at the man now walking toward us.

He started to say more in French but I asked him in Vietnamese if this was indeed Phu Văn Lâu. His face lit up. He turned to his compatriots still sitting by their picnic and repeated what I had said.

Then, without any announcement, he startled us by singing. He was singing the poem written by Ưng Bình for King Duy Tân, and for a Vietnam that was already vanishing a hundred years ago. With a gulp in my throat, I watched him sing. I saw his stubs of bad front teeth, stained brown from a lifetime of unfiltered cigarettes, and his eyes, the whites a bit rheumy. I thought of all that a man his age must have seen and endured and of the whimsical play alive in him that made him sing this poem because foreigners had come along and asked about Phu Văn Lâu in Vietnamese.

Then, to my further surprise, I joined him in singing, saying some of the phrases because I too knew the little poem by heart, having played my tape of it often, just as I had heard Mr. Hảo sing into my tape recorder decades before.

The other retirees got up to move closer, one woman using a cane. American tourists were no longer unusual in Huế. This was.

When the man stopped singing, he began to weep. His elderly companions said some words to comfort him. I looked at my wife and she was crying and then I started to tear up. I looked at our daughter who, at twenty-one, shared none of our memories of war, its destructions, or the peculiar, restorative beauty of this little poem. In this way, she was no different than most Americans or, indeed, most Vietnamese alive today, the majority born after the end of the war.

But wars, as we continue to forget, do not end when the last shot is fired. The hostile nations, winners and losers, are changed forever as soldiers come back altered, damaged, or not at all. Their families are changed forever. Slowly or quickly, these changes reverberate through society as the economic and personal costs continue to be paid long after the shooting is over and, out in the wider world, geopolitical delineations are reconfigured. The bigger the war, the greater the perturbations. In ancient China, generals returning home with their armies reentered the capital through a so-called Gate of Mourning. This was true whether the campaign had been a success or a defeat. The gate can be narrow, even just a moment that one passes through, forever altering one's path . . . like hearing a woman off by herself in an orchard and singing a poem, or encountering an old man sitting by a river singing a poem about a king and his kingdom gone long ago.

"What was *that* about?" our daughter asked, after everyone had recomposed themselves and shaken hands and we were walking back to our waiting taxi.

"A poem," I said, "from long ago."

NOTES

1. *Ca dao* (pronounced "ka zow" or "ka yow") is a term borrowed from the Chinese "Ko Yao" (歌 謠), "song and ballads." Much of Vietnamese literary terminology has been borrowed from Chinese in the way that English has borrowed from, say, classical Greek or Renaissance Italian. *Ca dao* themselves are purely Vietnamese in origin. For a fuller discussion and many more poems, see my *Ca Dao Việt Nam: Vietnamese Folk Poetry* (Copper Canyon Press, 2003).

2. See David Thomas and Robert K. Headley Jr., "More on Mon-Khmer Subgroupings," *Lingua* 25 (1970): 398–418, p. 404.

3. In my *Ca Dao Việt Nam* I took care to break lines *as sung* and to leave in any "extra" syllables inserted deliberately or by accident, rather than normalize the forms. I gave them titles in English, since in Vietnamese, they have none.

4. Solange Corbin, "La cantillation des rituels chrétiens," *Revue de musicologie* XLVII (July 1961): pp. 3–36. For application to Vietnamese music, see Trần Văn Khê, "Musique bouddhique du Viêtnam," in Jacques Porte, *Encyclopédie des musiques sacrées* (Labergerie, 1968), pp. 222–240.

5. Lê Thành Khôi "La chanson populaire vietnamienne," *Lettres nouvelles* (March 1954), p. 430. Dương Đình Khuê, *La littérature populaire vietnamienne,* (Thanh-Long, 1976), p. iii. Trịnh Huy Tiến, *La personnalité culturelle du Viêtnam,* (Ministère des affaires culturelles et sociales, 1969), p. 30.

6. Jeanne Cuisinier, *Les Mường* (Institut d'Ethnologie, Univ. Paris, 1946), pp. 446 and 562–569. See also Nguyễn Tu Chi, "A Mường Sketch," *Vietnamese Studies* no. 32, Ethnographic Data, vol. 1 (xunhasaba, 1972), p. 67. Lê Văn Hảo, "Ethnological Studies and Researches in North Vietnam," *Vietnamese Studies* no. 32, Ethnographic Data, vol. 1, p. 15.

7. For a more detailed discussion of this and other questions of development, see my "Vietnamese Oral Poetry," *Literature, East & West* XVI, no. 4 (April 1975), pp. 1217–1243.

8. To hear this and some other *ca dao,* go to www.johnbalaban.com and click on the Ca Dao Audio tab. See also: *Narrative:* https://narri.tv/2EJJPkW. Also, my 1971–1972 notebooks and recordings are now archived at the Harry Ransom Center at the University of Texas, Austin, and open to scholars.

9. 敷 phu meaning "to write," 文 văn meaning "literature," and 樓 lâu meaning "building" are the three characters still inscribed over the entrance: Phu Văn Lâu. King Duy Tân's moon-watching pavilion is on the Perfume River in Huế. The young king led a brief rebellion against the French. This *ca dao* is the only one in the book with a literary author: Ưng Bình, pen name "Thúc Giạ Thị." (See Nguyễn Du, *Truyện Kiều,* Chapter VIII, line 138.) Sometimes literary figures succeeded at inserting poems into the oral tradition, in this case an attempt to stir sentiment for the absent king pursued by French authorities.

10. Pierre Daudin, "Poèmes anacycliques de l'Empereur Thieu-Tri," *Bulletin de la Societé des Études Indochinoises* 47, no. 1 (1972): 2–24; 49, no. 2 (1974): 226–51.

Some *Ca Dao* Recorded in Vietnam, 1971–1972

The Sàigòn River

The Sàigòn River slides past the Old Market,
its broad waters thick with silt. There
the rice shoots gather a fragrance,
the fragrance of my country home,
recalling my motherhome, stirring deep love.

Sông Sàigòn chảy dài Chợ Cũ,
Nước mênh mông nước đổ phù sa.
Ngọt ngào ngọn lúa bát ngát hương (thơm)
Hương lúa của quê nhà (hò hò);
Hướng về quê mẹ đậm đà tình thương.

At the Exiled King's River Pavilion

Evening, and all around the King's Pavilion
people are sitting, fishing, sad and grieving,
loving, in love, remembering, waiting, watching.
Whose boat plies the river mists
offering so many river songs
to move these mountains and rivers, our nation?

Trước bến Phu Văn Lâu

Chiều chiều trước bến Phu Văn Lâu.
Ai ngồi, ai câu, ai rầu, ai thảm,
Ai thương, ai cảm, ai nhớ, ai đợi, ai trông.
Thuyền ai thấp thoáng bến sông,
Đưa chi nhiều câu mái đẩy,
Chạnh lòng nước non.

Leaving the Village

Even when cross planks are nailed down,
bamboo bridges are shaky, unsound. Hard going.
Hard going, so push on home to tidal flats to catch crab,
to the river for fish, to our sandy patch for melons.

Ví dầu cầu ván đóng đinh,
Cầu tre lắc lẻo gập ghình khó đi.
Khó đi, khó đẩy, về rẫy ăn cồng;
Về sông ăn cá, về giồng ăn dưa.

Love Lament

Stepping into the field: sadness fills my deep heart.
Bundling rice sheaves: tears dart in two streaks.
Who made me miss the ferry's leaving?
Who made this shallow creek that parts both sides?

Bước xuống ruộng sâu man sầu tấc dạ.
Tay ôm bó mạ nước mắt hai hàng.
Ai làm lỡ chuyến đò ngang.
Cho biệt ly sông cạn nước đôi đàng.

The Red Cloth

Sad, idle, I think of my dead mother,
her mouth chewing rice, her tongue removing fish bones.

The Red Cloth drapes the mirror frame.
Men of one country should love one another.

Ngồi buồn nhớ mẹ ta xưa:
Miệng nhai cơm trắng lưỡi lừa cá xương.
Nhiễu điều phủ lấy giá gương.
Người trong một nước phải thương nhau cùng.

The Ship of Redemption

The bell of Linh Mụ Pagoda tolls,
awakening the drowsy soul,
probing, reminding us of karmic debt,
washing us clean of worldly dust.
A boat crosses to the Western Peace.

Thức tỉnh hồn mê tiếng chuông Linh Mụ,
Dặn dò nợ trần duyên rửa sạch.
Qua đò đã tây phương.

A Tiny Bird

A tiny bird with red feathers,
a tiny bird with black beak
drinks up the lotus pond day by day.
Perhaps I must leave you.

Con chim nho nhỏ,
Cái lông nó đỏ,
Cái mỏ nó đen,
Nó uống nước ao sen ngày cạn.
Cơ hội này anh đành đoạn bỏ em.

Tao

Sad, I blame Mister Sky.
When sad, I laugh. Happy, I cry.
Not a man, in my next life
I'll become a rustling pine
on a cliff in the sky.
Fly with the pines, cool and lonely.

Ngồi buồn trách lẫn ông xanh,
Khi vui muốn khóc, buồn tênh lại cười.
Kiếp sau xin chớ làm người,
Làm cây thông đứng giữa trời mà reo.
Giữa trời vách đá cheo-leo,
Ai mà chịu rét thì trèo với thông.

The Arranged Marriage

Mother wanted the dowry of rice,
the huge sow, and Cảnh-Hưng coins,
although I asked her to refuse.
She raved and ranted and made the match.
So now one is low; the other, high.
Like unmatched chopsticks, never equal.

Mẹ em tham thúng xôi đền,
Tham con lợn béo, tham tiền Cảnh-Hưng.
Tôi đã bảo mẹ rằng đừng,
Mẹ hầm, mẹ hứ, mẹ bưng ngay vào.
Bây giờ kẻ thấp, người cao,
Như đôi đũa lệch, so sao cho bằng.

The Outpost Soldier

Here are only cliffs and crags,
bird tracks, beasts shuffling, locusts chirring,
and jungle trees rustling their music.
A bird calls out from a gnarled tree.
I've lived in the forest for three years.

Ở đây những núi cùng khe,
Chân chim bóng thú, tiếng ve gọi sầu.
Ngàn lim ve vẩy khúc cầm,
Gốc cây cổ thụ tiếng chim vang lừng.
Ba năm ăn ở trên rừng.

Spring Essence: The Poetry of Hồ Xuân Hương

Hồ Xuân Hương—her given name means "Spring Essence" or "Spring Perfume"—was born around 1780 at the end of the second Lê dynasty, a period of calamity and social disintegration. Her fame in Vietnam as a poet and cultural figure continues to this day. A concubine, although a high-ranking one, she followed Chinese classical forms in her poetry, but preferred to write not in Chinese but in *chữ Nôm*, "the Southern Characters" that represented Vietnamese speech. And while her prosody followed traditional Chinese classical forms, her poems were anything but conventional. Whether about mountain landscapes, or longings after love, or apparently about such common things as a fan, weaving, some fruit, or even a river snail, many of her poems were devilish double entendres with hidden sexual meaning, albeit in a Confucian tradition of propriety that banished the nude from art. Writing about sex was unheard of. And, if this were not enough to incur disfavor in a time when impropriety was punished by the sword, she wrote poems that ridiculed the authority of the decaying Buddhist church, the feudal state, and Confucian male society. Yet, because of her stunning poetic cleverness, she and her poems survived. Young scholar-poets strived to match wits with her. Her poems were copied by hand for almost a hundred years before they finally saw a woodblock printing in 1909.

My *Spring Essence: The Poetry of Hồ Xuân Hương* was the first printing of her collected poetry in any Western language. Indeed, it was the first time that her poems had been actually *printed* in TrueType fonts and in the Nôm she wrote in, rather than passed on by hand or copied in limited woodblock editions. Indeed, 1,000 years of Nôm writing—in literature, law, religion, government, medicine, and philosophy—were long unreachable to all but a handful of Vietnamese scholars who could still read this calligraphic writing system, which began its slow surrender to Western-style, roman alphabetic script toward the end of the seventeenth century. *Spring Essence* was a first step, through digital coding, toward recovering this long literary tradition.

Autumn Landscape

Drop by drop rain slaps the banana leaves.
Praise whoever sketched this desolate scene:

the lush, dark canopies of the gnarled trees,
the long river, sliding smooth and white.

I lift my wine flask, drunk with rivers and hills.
My backpack, breathing moonlight, sags with poems.

Look, and love everyone.
Whoever sees this landscape is stunned.

Cảnh thu

Thánh thót tầu tiêu mấy hạt mưa,
Khen ai khéo vẽ cảnh tiêu sơ.
Xanh om cổ thụ tròn xoe tán,
Trắng xoá tràng giang phẳng lặng tờ.
Bầu dốc giang sơn say chấp rượu,
Túi lưng phong nguyệt nặng vì thơ.
Ơ hay, cảnh cũng ưa người nhỉ,
Ai thấy, ai mà chẳng ngẩn ngơ.

景秋

聖淬艚簫余紇𩅹
𠸦埃窖𦘧景消疎
撐菩古樹𠁀𡂞傘
𤽸𢭂長江滂朗詞
瓢篤江山醝執𨢇
褸𦡟風月礦爲詩
於咍景拱㤇得吀
埃𧡊埃𠸍庄謹𢠩

Offering Betel

A piece of nut and a bit of leaf.
Here, Xuân Hương has smeared it.

If love is fated, you'll chew it red,
Lime won't stay white, nor leaf, green.

Mời ăn trầu

Quả cau nho nhỏ miếng trầu hôi
Này của Xuân Hương mới quệt rồi
Có phải duyên nhau thời thắm lại
Đừng xanh như lá bạc như vôi.

哜哎莆

菓橰儒㧄㕇莆灰
尼貼春香買捑末
固沛緣饒辰糁吏
停撑如蘆泊如硙

On Sharing a Husband

Screw the fate that makes you share a man.
One cuddles under cotton blankets; the other's cold.

Every now and then, well, maybe or maybe not,
once or twice a month, oh, it's like nothing.

You try to stick to it like a fly on rice
but the rice is rotten. You slave like the maid,

but without pay. If I had known how it would go
I think I would have lived alone.

Lấy chồng chung

Chém cha cái kiếp lấy chồng chung
Kẻ đắp chăn bông kẻ lạnh lùng
Năm thì mười hoạ hay chăng chớ
Một tháng đôi lần có cũng không
Cố bám ăn xôi xôi lại hỏng
Cầm bằng làm mướn mướn không công
Thân này ví biết dường này nhỉ
Thà trước thôi đành ở vậy xong.

祕斁終

刦吒丐刦祕斁終　　故擃哰欤欤吏吼
几搭禛蒽几泠凁　　拎朋𢚁擾擾空功
舡時迠匾咍庄𥙩　　身尼喈別羕尼㖧
没腩堆吝固悑空　　他戳催停於丕衝

Jackfruit

My body is like the jackfruit on the branch:
my skin is coarse, my meat is thick.

Kind sir, if you love me, pierce me with your stick.
Caress me and sap will slicken your hands.

Quả mít

Thân em như quả mít trên cây
Da nó xù xì, múi nó dầy.
Quân tử có yêu thì đóng cọc,
Xin đừng mân mó, nhựa ra tay.

菓樲

身媕如菓樲蓮橤
膠奴夠仕胹奴觳
君子固腰辰揀樐
吖停縖揲涵審秕

River Snail

Fate and my parents shaped me like a snail,
day and night wandering marsh weeds that smell foul.

Kind sir, if you want me, open my door.
But please don't poke up into my tail.

Vịnh ốc nhồi

Bác mẹ sinh ra phận ốc nhồi
Đêm ngày lăn lóc đám cỏ hôi
Quân tử có thương thì bóc yếm
Xin đừng ngó ngoáy lỗ trôn tôi.

詠屋蛛

博媟生番分屋蛛
腚哷舛跙盎鞈灰
君子固傷辰扑穊
吀停扞揆魯膵碎

Three Mountain Pass

A cliff face. Another. And still a third.
Who was so skilled to carve this craggy scene:

the cavern's red door, the ridge's narrow cleft,
the black knoll bearded with little mosses?

A twisting pine bough plunges in the wind,
showering a willow's leaves with glistening drops.

Gentlemen, lords, who could refuse, though weary
and shaky in his knees, to mount once more?

Đèo Ba Dội

Một đèo, một đèo, lại một đèo,
Khen ai khéo tạc cảnh cheo leo.
Cửa son đỏ loét tùm hum nóc,
Hòn đá xanh rì lún phún rêu.
Lắt lẻo cành thông cơn gió thốc,
Đầm đìa lá liễu giọt sương gieo.
Hiền nhân, quân tử ai mà chẳng . . .
Mỏi gối, chồn chân vẫn muốn trèo.

岊岯隊

没岊没岊吏没岊　　　　　揍跒梗椿干鑓速
唒埃窖鑿景招撩　　　　　潭濙蘿柳淐霜招
靯輪霵烈筬歓窟　　　　　賢人君子埃嚅挭
圿硺撑黃頓噴蒌　　　　　痳蹖痳蹎吻愵蹣

Confession (I)

Gray sky. A rooster crows.
Bitter, I look out on thickets and folds.

I haven't shook grief's rattle, yet it clatters.
I haven't rung sorrow's bell, though it tolls.

Their noise only drags me down, angry
with a fate that says I'm much too bold.

Men of talent, learned men, where are you?
Am I supposed to walk as if stooped and old?

Tự tình thơ

Tiếng gà xao xác gáy trên bom
Oán hận trông ra khắp mọi chòm
Mõ thảm không khua mà cũng cốc
Chuông sầu chẳng đánh cớ sao om
Trước nghe những tiếng thêm rầu rĩ
Sau giận vì duyên để mõm mòm
Tài tử văn nhân ai đó tá
Thân này đã hẳn chịu già hom.

叙情詩

㗂鴚嗃唴嘅𨕭𡀔
怨恨瞳𨖅泣每笭
楳慘空摳𪇌哄谷
鐘愁拯打攎𩍢喑
𧼋䁨仍㗂添油忋
𢴐悚為緣底㗼䐢
才子文人埃㧣佐
身尼㐌罕𠺥䊷悎

Teasing Chiêu-Hổ

Is the master drunk? Is the master awake?
Why flirt with the moon in the middle of the day?

Perhaps there's something I ought to say:
Don't stick your hand in the tiger's cave.

Cợt ông Chiêu-Hổ

Anh đồ tỉnh anh đồ say
Sao anh ghẹo nguyệt giữa ban ngày
Này này chị bảo cho mà biết
Chốn ấy hang hùm chớ mó tay.

吃翁昭虎

英徒醒英徒醛
翗英撟月𦝄班唭
尼尼姉㗭朱礝別
准意酨猞藩揲𥬧

Weaving at Night

Lampwick turned up, the room glows white.
The loom moves easily all night long

as feet work and push below.
Nimbly the shuttle flies in and out,

wide or narrow, big or small, sliding in snug.
Long or short, it glides out smoothly.

Girls who do it right, let it soak
then wait a while for the blush to show.

Dệt cửi

Thắp ngọn đèn lên thấy trắng phau;
Con cò mấp máy suốt đêm thâu.
Hai chân đạp xuống năng năng nhắc,
Một suốt đâm ngang thích thích mau.
Rộng, hẹp, nhỏ, to vừa vặn cả,
Ngắn, dài, khuôn khổ vẫn như nhau.
Cô nào muốn tốt ngâm cho kỹ,
Chờ đến ba thu mới dãi mầu.

継紴

熘院畑蓮筧皐抛	蘿狹毴蘇旇紊奇
琨鵞扡欂捽胮輪	鞔畏困苦沴如饒
台踸踖窀能能扡	姑市惘悴吟朱技
没捽抾昂適適毛	除旦巴秋買焴牟

The Paper Fan

Seventeen, or is it eighteen . . .
Ribs? Let me have it in my hands.

Thick or thin, opening its lovely angles.
Wide or narrow, inserted with a stick.

The hotter you get, the more refreshing.
Wonderful both night and day.

Cheeks juicy soft, persimmon pink.
Kings and lords just love this thing.

Vịnh quạt

Mười bẩy hay là mười tám đây
Cho anh yêu dấu chẳng rời tay
Mỏng dầy chừng ấy chành ba góc
Rộng hẹp dường nào cắm một cây
Càng nóng bao nhiêu thời càng mát
Yêu đêm chưa phỉ lại yêu ngày
Hồng hồng má phấn duyên vì cậy
Chúa dấu vua yêu một cái này.

詠𠡚

进罷咍羅进𤾓低　　強爌包饒辰強沬
朱英要踚庄淶疋　　要店諸斐吏要時
蒙𥢏程意撐𡾵𦊚　　紅紅𦟐粉緣為恄
藘狹樣庯悉沒核　　主踚希要没丐尼

The Floating Cake

My body is white; my fate, softly rounded,
rising and sinking like mountains in streams.

Whatever way hands may shape me,
at center my heart is red and true.

Bánh trôi

Thân em thì trắng, phận em tròn,
Bẩy nổi ba chìm mầy nước non.
Rắn nát mặc đầu tay kẻ nặn,
Mà em vẫn giữ tấm lòng son.

餅潭

身媕辰瓳分媕𦈱
罷浽㴜沉買渃嫩
硯湼默油𥱮几捏
𥱮媕刕竚沁悉輪

The Unwed Mother

Because I was too easy, this happened.
Can you guess the hollow in my heart?

Fate did not push out a bud
even though the willow grew.

He will carry this a hundred years
but I must bear the burden now.

Never mind the gossip of the world.
Don't have it, yet have it. So simple.

Vịnh người chửa hoang

Cả nể cho nên hoá dở dang
Nỗi lòng chàng có biết chăng chàng.
Duyên thiên chưa thấy nhô đầu dọc
Phận liễu sao đà đẩy nét ngang
Cái tội trăm năm chàng chịu cả
Chữ tình một khối thiếp xin mang
Quản bao miệng thế nhời chênh lệch
Không có, nhưng mà có, mấy ngoan.

詠得瀦荒

奇怵朱铖化揆揚　　丐罪耒觧払貂奇
餕悉払固別庄払　　竻情没塊姜吁拰
緣天渚筧儒頭育　　畓包呬世哩征壥
分了鞠色抯浧昂　　空固仍殤固買頑

Quán Sứ Pagoda

One wonders why Quán Sứ's so dead.
Ask for the abbot, you get no one.

The monks no longer beat the temple drum.
The nuns just say their beads and then are gone.

At morning light, no one struck the gong.
Late afternoon, the mossy walks undone.

To hell with life as snug as hand in glove.
This scene's made sadder by our debt of love.

Vịnh chùa Quán Sứ

Quán Sứ sao mà cảnh vắng teo
Hỏi thăm sư cụ đáo nơi neo
Chày kình tiểu để suông không đấm
Tràng hạt vãi lần đếm lại đeo
Sáng banh không kẻ khua tang mít
Trưa chật không ai móc kẽ rêu
Cha kiếp đường tu sao dắt díu
Cảnh buồn thêm ngán nợ tình đeo.

詠厨館使

館使䄂𥚯景永消	創𣈖空几摳喪橃
嗨嘇師具到坭扔	曓秩空埃抶技蓑
椻鯨小底忱空攇	吃刼塘修䋲撚掃
長曷娓㖖點吏扔	景愶添嗲嬾情扔

Trấn Quốc Temple

Weeds sprout outside the royal chapel.
I ache thinking of this country's past.

No incense swirls the Lotus Seat
curling across the king's robes

rising and falling wave upon wave.
A bell tolls. The past fades further.

Old heroes, old deeds, where are they?
One sees only this flock of shaved heads.

Vịnh chùa Trấn Quốc

Trấn Bắc hành cung cỏ dãi dầu
Chạnh niềm cố quốc nghĩ mà đau
Một toà sen toả hơi hương ngự
Năm thức mây phong nếp áo chầu
Sóng lớp phế hưng coi vẫn dộn
Chuông hồi kim cổ lắng càng mau
Người xưa cảnh cũ đâu đâu tá
Khéo ngẩn ngơ thay lũ trọc đầu.

詠厨鎮國

鎮北行宮鞊焣油	湙泣廢興豌沕嗺
懰念故國擬齌疠	鐘回今古聅彊毛
没座蓮鎖唏香御	侢智景斶兜兜佐
舿式霊封攝禩朝	窖謹魚台屡濁頭

Spring-Watching Pavilion

A gentle spring evening arrives
airily, unclouded by worldly dust.

Three times the bell tolls echoes like a wave.
We see heaven upside down in sad puddles.

Love's vast sea cannot be emptied.
And springs of grace flow easily everywhere.

Where is nirvana?
Nirvana is here, nine times out of ten.

Đài khán xuân

Êm ái, chiều xuân tới khán đài
Lâng lâng chẳng bợn chút trần ai.
Ba hồi chiêu mộ chuông gầm song.
Một vũng tang thương nước lộn trời.
Bể ái nghìn trùng khôn tát cạn.
Nguồn ân muôn trượng dễ khơi vơi.
Nào nào cực lạc là đâu tá?
Cực lạc là đây, chín rõ mười.

檯看春

淹愛朝春細看檯　　波愛舒重坤撒泲
凌凌庄泲虬塵埃　　源恩閣丈褪澗潙
屵回招墓鍾哗湧　　鬧鬧極樂羅兜佐
没潷喪滄洺論歪　　極樂羅低尨燴迊

*They asked the traveler where he came
from, where he was going.
He replied, "I am coming from behind my back,
going in the direction I am facing."*
THE HUNDRED THOUSAND SONGS
OF MILAREPA

Christmas Eve at Washington's Crossing

Out on the freezing Delaware, ice sheets bob the surface, breaking
against granite pilings of the colonial river inn swept by winter storm.

Gusts of snow blow off a sandbar and sink in plunging currents
where a line of ducks paddles hard against the blizzard

as cornfields on the Jersey banks are whisked into bits
of stalks and broken sheaves spinning in the squalls.

This is where, one such Christmas night, the tall courtly general with bad teeth
risked his neck and his rebels to cross the storming river and rout the Hessians.

What made them think they could succeed? . . . farmers mostly,
leaving homesteads to load cannon into Durham boats

to row into the snowstorm, then march all night to Trenton,
saving the Republic for Valley Forge and victory at Yorktown.

Before crossing, legend says, they assembled in the snow to hear
Paine's new essay about summer soldiers and sunshine patriots.

What words could call us all together now? On what riverbank?
For what common good would we abandon all?

Highway 61 Revisited

Summer was flooding the city highways
bathing sycamores below the savage tenements,
leafage flushed green, almost obscuring
the plastic grocery bags snagged in branch-tops
flapping in the roadside wind, in the whine
of semis and buses and cars and vans
plastic shreds fluttering, prayer flags of the poor,
as rackety apartment ACs hummed an *AUM* chorus
in the June cement heat, and I sped by, heading out
once more for the heart of the heart of the country,
rolling down Highway 61, heading West and South,
lighting out again, away from fanfare and drumbeats,
the couples holding hands in their slow-motion leaps
from the skyscraper windows billowing smoke.

In Midwestern farmlands rustling wheatcrowns,
spreading out with alfalfa and sorghum, sprouting corn,
I thought I was lost, in the crickets and songbirds,
but tire whine and bumper glare kept me on course
and when I picked up the soldier mugged in the bus station,
teeth kicked in, wallet taken, hitching back to base in Waco
to his tank-repair unit readying for another Iraq war
I knew I was on the right road, running like a lifeline
across the palm of America.

                         In Texas, I heard voices.
In the dead-ugly creosote basin of Midland–Odessa
where—all across the hot mesquite horizon—oil jockeys
pumped crude from the sandy wastes, and a billboard
boasted, "Home of President and Mrs. George W. Bush."
I had a powerful urge to pee and pulled off the highway.

Taking my whiz at an Exxon, then gassing up again,
I looked around when I heard a voice calling, "Help me."
Calling softly, "Can you help me?" I looked around
and saw an elderly man in a battered Honda, door open,
big shoes planted on the greasy cement, looking at me.
"What do you need?" I asked, thinking maybe a few bucks,
but he wanted me to *lift his legs* into his little car.
Prosthetic legs, I could feel, heavy as cinder blocks.
"Where you headed?" I asked, as he turned the key,
but he just pointed his finger like a gun, said
"*That* way, down Highway 61."

I turned onto a less traveled blacktop running south
past volcanic peaks to Mexico and the Big Bend.
From my windshield to the horizon, dust devils
swirled over the greasewood and yucca spikes,
whipping up little tornadoes of dust and grit
around the odd horse or pronghorns grazing with cattle
behind hundreds of miles of barbed-wire fences—a dry land,
old haunt of raiding Apaches, Comanches, Pancho Villa.

But tonight is the summer solstice and I am with friends
in this high-desert border town rumbled by freight trains.
Outside the moon has risen over the Sierra Madres,
shining on burros shuffling through willows, below cottonwoods
along the Rio Grande, glistening on the backs of thumb-size
toads in the stone pans where water seeps in the canyons,
shining on the humble folk wading into Texas,
shining on the Border Patrols, on the DEA blimp,
shining on the bright empty ribbon of Highway 61,
loud with strange cries echoing across America.

Sotol

Miles of barbed wire strung to the horizon
fencing cattle and their graze of greasewood
puckered with yellow blossoms, scattered
with dry grasses, cat's claw, thistle, spurge,
fan-strands of spiny ocotillo, mescal, mesquite,
fishhook and prickly pear cactus, acacia, yucca
and sotol spikes spraying white blossoms.

Along a fence line: a passel of turkey vultures
perch, wings spread, taking the sun into
their black capes, these mask-of-red-death
horrors, their faces wattled in bluish warts, waiting
for the dead—pronghorn or jackrabbit, luck
run out, or maybe a boy from across the border.

Yet on this early morning yellow warblers
trill the desert willows along the arroyo.
Even the cottonwoods are taking off in song,
trembling great leafy tambourines in the cool air
while down by the Rio, a Border Patrol SUV
is dragging a sledge of old tires through a dry wash,
sweeping footprints for a day of tracking aliens.

Mexicans make a drink from sotol
something like tequila or pulque from maguey,
an elixir of agave, a tincture of spike and thorn,
distilled from sun and wheeling shadows,
with a pinch of cactus bloom, a scent of sage.
A strong, perplexing drink: Birdsong
at the first sip. Thorn in the tongue, at the last.
And yet we drink. And drink again.

The Lives of the Poets

The country is proud of its dead poets. It takes terrific satisfaction
in the poets' testimony that the USA is too tough, too big, too much,
too rugged, that American reality is overpowering. . . . So poets
are loved, but loved because they just can't make it here.

    SAUL BELLOW, *HUMBOLDT'S GIFT*

Fact is, it's a reality that grinds us all,
even those who whisper to themselves: *If* I
were not such a corrupt, unfeeling bastard, creep,
thief, and vulture, I couldn't get through this either.
Still they collapse at meetings, on tennis courts,
pig valves going kaboom in their hearts,
pitching into their *Wall Street Journals*
as the train lurches home to the Hamptons,
as the cab crawls uptown to the condo on the Park.
Dying in their dandruff, on their treadmills,
taking their sips of dioxin seepage,
eyes fried by computer screens and boredom.
The huge need for cocaine said it all.

Well, these were the thoughts that came to me
on a high wooded bluff outside Port Townsend
just after Levertov died. Her *Times* obit
ran next to some admiral's from the Vietnam War,
apparent adversaries, now side by side,
true to their conflicting truths.
The hand that gives. The hand that takes.

All about me clumps of sweet pea, purples
and pinks, cascaded down the grassy hillsides

All italicized quotes are from Saul Bellow, *Humboldt's Gift* (Viking, 1975), p. 117.

as dawn mist raveled a wreath through inky tops
of Douglas firs. Far off, the distant Strait
of Juan de Fuca pulled tides below a cloudbank
and ferry foghorns called, each to each.
Can sung words calm the guns of a steeled fleet?
(*Orpheus moved stones and trees. But a poet
can't perform a hysterectomy or send a vehicle
out of the solar system.*) At Sotheby's,
Ginsberg's top hat went for $258 after
the bad gray poet launched his last exhalation.

Unsettled, I drove to Seattle's Blue Moon Tavern
where soon I annoyed a man with straggly hair
and baseball cap, reading Cicero through wire-rims,
hunched at the beat-up bar and railing at me,
"Man, I *told* you. I don't *know* those people!"
My mistake. He looked like he might have
perched on that barstool reading Latin
for decades since abandoning a dissertation.
But he didn't know Roethke, or Hugo, or Wright,
whose framed lugubrious black and whites
still hung from the rough plank walls
where once they drank and howled like Humboldt.
The only woman among them: Carolyn Kizer,
with her huge sultry eyes and severe French hat,
Dorothy Parker to this Algonquin of moonstruck boozers.

*The weakness of the spiritual powers is proved
in the childishness, madness, drunkenness, and despair
of these martyrs. . . . They succumbed, poor loonies.*
One thinks of Roethke weeping over a dead mouse
cupped in his huge hands. Of Hugo sweating out
a hangover in the bleachers of a sandlot game.

Lew Welch walking off forever into the scorpion Sierras.
Hart Crane over the side of a ship. And Jarrell
falling in front of a car. And poor John Berryman
jumping from a bridge. (And Plath and Sexton
gassing themselves.) Delmore Schwartz,
Humboldt Humbert, shouting from the moon.

— ⸺

So, praise to those still coming through on song,
a bigger tribe than one can name and tough
as anything put up by corporate America:
Maxine Kumin with her horse-broke neck, still
writing, still hitching up and riding Deuter.
William Meredith struggling back toward speech.
Hayden Carruth raising a toast with his "poet's
cheap, sufficient Chardonnay." Richard Wilbur
calling us to morning air awash with angels.
Merwin in Hawaii, Snyder in the Sierras,
both taking the nothingness of *sunyata*
to conjure up a habitation.
                              Walking
their Sonoma farm with Kizer's husband John,
we stopped before a storm-struck, twisted pear tree,
a remnant from an orchard of 100 years ago.
Out of the hulk of its blackened trunk,
one smooth-skinned branch sent forth some leaves.
"Still blooming?" I asked. "Madly," he said.

Loving Graham Greene

for Gloria Emerson

*But in Indochina I drained a magic potion, a loving cup which I
have shared since with many retired* colons *and officers of the Foreign
Legion, whose eyes light up at the mention of Saigon and Hanoi.*
GRAHAM GREENE, *WAYS OF ESCAPE*

So there he was, decades after the war,
rattled and adrift, waiting in the waiting room
of a shrink in New Mexico, of all places,

an office in a garden by an adobe house
its tin roof aflame with sunlight
as the sun humped across blue sky

and hummingbirds raced to plunder heads
of purple cosmos and bee balm while sunflowers
looked up like a congregation seeking benediction.

Beyond the garden, the river surged over
canyon rocks and piñon snags where big trout
lurked in the cold shadows of dark pools.

He was on vacation; he hadn't planned this visit.
The wife and kids were taking the trail ride.
He had found the name in the phone book.

After a lot of babble and blubbering, the guy
asked him if he knew what was wrong,
what was hurting him so, why he was crying,

why he was here. He shook
his head "no." No,
he didn't know.

"Still a reporter?" *Yes.*
"Successful?" *Yes, pretty much.*
"Happily married?" *Well, yeah.*

"But your eyes," he said, "are dead,
except when you mention Vietnam
and then a little spurt of epinephrine

zings your system and your eyes light up."
The therapist charged sixty bucks,
suggested he take up skydiving.

Driving back to the riddled heap of villagers
from which someone had pulled out a live 3-year-old,
past the berm wire where they were still yanking off

the bodies, he was flying in a chopper when it dove down
to open up on a lone elephant in a field of sugarcane.
After a gin fizz on the veranda of the Continental Palace,

he was back at the motel where everyone was by the pool,
the kids all lit up after their trail ride high on the canyon rim,
where the air was sweet with pine and bear grass, the sky clear.

Some Dogs of the World

VENICE BEACH, CALIFORNIA

Out there, waves wobble up and crash in sunglare.
And here: rows of tattoo parlors, sunglass stands,
tanned babes and oiled boys sweeping by on Rollerblades,
past tourists, palm readers, ice-cream parlors, the air alive
with Carlos Santana whose "Black Magic Woman"
is wiggling her middle-aged butt through a loudspeaker
as two leathery blondes sashay out from the '60s
—one with daisies pinned to her beret, the other with ribbons
fluttering from her graying hair and a smile pinned on
for the sunstruck shuffle of T-shirted tourists in shorts
pausing now to gawk at a high-heeled *donna alla moda*
walking her Chihuahua like a rat on a rope.

CLUJ, TRANSYLVANIA, ROMANIA

Outside the Panegrano Patiserie
a man with greasy jacket and beret
feeds two strays some bits of sweet roll.
One mutt chews the bread thoughtfully.
This isn't what she was looking for, but it's food,
and the nice, smelly man is laughing.
Then her mate takes off howling
after a third dog trotting down the street,
chasing the interloper helter-skelter
through legs of passersby, barking
and yammering, bowling over some guy
like a set of tenpins. The whole street's shouting
in Magyar and Romanian. And the dogs scatter.
Later, on the road to Bucharest, a bay horse
lies dead in the roadside gravel

where a Gypsy cart got smashed by a car,
a wild dog yanking at its tail and hocks.

LUNCH WITH A DISTRICT CHIEF, OUTSIDE HANOI

My American friend, who is vegetarian but making concessions,
thinks the translator said, "Can you eat dark meat?"
But, of course, it is "dog," not *dark*. Puppy, not *poulet*.
By the third or fourth bite, the translation is corrected,
and my friend swallows, smiles, and says it's good
out of deference to our host, a decent man
who was shot through the lungs during our war,
who was sent home to die, and who now is smiling
at the chance, at last, to talk to these Americans.

PARIS, LE PETIT ZINC RESTAURANT

Fancy people. Fancy food.
And here comes Spot bopping along
la rue Buci, a veritable boulevardier
pausing to lift a hind leg and pee, while cocking
one admiring eye on the elegant sidewalk diners.
Ah, *mes semblables.*

On the Death of his Dog, Apples

No mair to wander through the glen
And disturb the peace of the pheasant hen.
OLD SCOTTISH SONG

Old mutt, asleep on your rug
but game into dotage
you'd sometimes yelp and work your legs
running rabbits in dreamland.

Thinned to bone by a bellyful of cancer,
when the vet syringed your shaved vein
you looked at me as if we'd flushed a grouse,
ears perked, eyes startled.

And when your eyes fogged
and your muzzle slumped in the crook of my arm,
I dreamed for you an upland meadow,
a clear brook of bright water,

hillsides full of pheasants
where rabbits frisked in bluebells,
where you dozed then rose to greet me
wagging your tail as I crossed the creek.

Soldier Home

At first Krebs . . . did not want to talk about the war at all.
Later he felt the need to talk but no one wanted to hear about it.
ERNEST HEMINGWAY, "SOLDIER'S HOME"

Full moon over Beaufort Inlet, moon path streaming toward him
barefoot on the cold beach, watching wave crests rush the shore.

Out in the Atlantic silence, boat lights wink on a black horizon
as a Camp Lejeune chopper circles and circles a spot on the sea,

engine staccato louder than the waves, searchlights
brighter than the moon. Finally it breaks off, heads landward,

a wasp shape bisecting the moon, lights cut at the shoreline,
engine loud in the boy's head. Not even the waves can drown it.

"Captains and soldiers are smeared on the bushes and grass;
Our generals schemed in vain," Li Po wrote, twelve centuries ago.

If Only

Their cottage sat on a grassy bluff
weathered by salt spray, fogs, and rain
blowing off dunes and bleached logpiles
past tidal creeks seeping out to sea.

Cattails bobbed with redwing blackbirds.
Sparrows clamored through wild-rose thickets.
Two dogs, spattered with sandy muck,
snoozed on the sunny porch steps.

Dinner simmered on the stove.
Pulling weeds in the garden, she smiled,
hearing his tires pop gravel and clamshells
at their rutted lane's long winding end.

The dogs leapt up, loped out to greet him.
This is how it should have been.

Leaving

All her hopes
    were in the house
she was walking out of
    shutting the screen door
as the kitchen flared
    in smoke
of shouts and kisses,
    laughter, cooking, cleaning,
and, then, just
    the old, exhausting quarrels,
the wrangling, the accusations—
    while, inside,
the addled man sat on a stool,
    dying for a drink,
flames on his glasses,
    plucking his amplified guitar
as the windows flashed
    conflagrations
                of lost wishes.

Out by the curb
    in the backseat
packed with clothes and books
    her goofy setter
looked bewildered;
    her sad Lab
hung his chin out the window.

Behind their curtains
    neighbors watched

having said the proper things;
    the little girl
she sometimes minded
    was still crying
as her mother encouraged her
    to wave goodbye.

All along the shady street
    maple seeds let loose
and spun to the ground.
    All her hopes
had been in that house
    that she was driving away from,
maple seeds fluttering down,
    guitar fading,
    the road to Somewhere
    opening ahead.

The Goodbyes

What have I become,
my sweetest friend?
Everyone I know
goes away in the end.

JOHNNY CASH, SINGING TRENT REZNOR'S "HURT"

Our last farewells may come as a surprise.
Whether we made our preparations, or never bothered.

For some, it's *au revoir;* for others, just goodbye.
Or "oops" or even "no!" but, still, a final moment of *me.*

Losing others goes on longer, both the dead and alive
Who we will never see again but in dream or memory.

Whisper their names into your pillow at bedtime.
Say them all you want, you are calling after ghosts:

Dead parents, good or bad, dwelling in terminal silence.
Ex's living in Ohio with someone you've never met.

Past lovers, old friends, homes you had, last replies.
Lips you kissed, would kiss again. Children grown and gone.

This is our harder trial; these, our bleakest times:
Not our own going, but the going of others.

Driving Back East with My Dad

I still see him through the Instamatic, standing
before the Great Sand Dunes of the southern Rockies,
a slow wind pulling streams of sand across his knees
as the dunes loomed behind him and he squinted
at the camera, baseball cap over his long white hair.
Seventy-five, and about to ride 2,000 miles in my old pickup.

In his Romanian village, he is still remembered
for making, age 12, a die for counterfeiting coins.
At 14, not that long after the Wright brothers
and Kitty Hawk, he flew his model plane
over the cornfields of his Schwabe neighbors.
In his village of geese and corn bins, he studied calculus.
Once, he saved a boy nearly pecked to death by geese.
By 18, he was a roundhouse foreman in the Carpathians.
At 19, swimming the Danube to an island where Turks
sold their heavenly tobacco, he almost drowned
until a Tatar girl jumped in to haul him out.

At 21, he came here with scarcely a word of English,
joined the US Army as a Cavalry officer, but was obliged
to resign his commission for clobbering his superior
with a weighted riding crop. In World War II,
working at the Philadelphia Naval Yard, he invented
the C130 "Flying Boxcar." (I still have his blueprints.)
After the war, in Scranton, lunching with his staff of engineers,
he made them march out of the Purple Cow restaurant
when the maître d' wouldn't serve his Black draftsman.
One of his inventions—a step ladder/ironing board/high chair
—got us on a '50s TV show called *The Big Idea,*
where I climbed up in the high chair in my little suit.

He went bankrupt; had a wicked temper,
once mortifying my mother by tossing her bowl of soup
into a rude waiter's face, and chasing him into the kitchen.
At 16, after one of his punch-ups, I ran away from home.

Can't say we said much on our drive,
a mere detour on his long crooked path.
As the miles rolled past, we only stopped
for diner food, gas, and motels where we'd sip
his Jack Daniel's and watch TV from our beds.
Five days of driving, with a biblical start:
black skies slamming down thunder,
rips of lightning, and even a tornado
that churned up a wheat field near Limon
as we rattled along into Kansas,
hail whacking my truck, thumping off
the cab and hood and clattering the back bed with ice.
He just turned off his hearing aid, and Sphinx-like
seemed pleased with his ride through the high plains.

How I wish for a lyric ending to this prose tale:
a moment when the travelers, going in the direction
they faced, found they had already arrived. Still,
it was good, being alive together, taking in the road,
mindful of where we had come, and moving on.

Dinner in Miami

We may live without friends; we may live without books; but civilized men cannot live without cooks.

EDWARD ROBERT BULWER, EARL OF LYTTON, *LUCILE*

ENTRÉE

The worn-out man and his red-eyed wife
had driven up from the Keys at the end of an awful day
spent wrangling with a son, bankrupt once again.
It might have perked them up, had they known
their chef once cooked for Princess Grace.
Maybe not. "You are what you eat. Eat what you are,"
the man declared, downing his stiff drink to order
the bourbon-soaked rib eye with orange chimichurri.
His wife sighed and could not decide
between the Key West yellowtail
and the cassoulet with confit of duck.

Their lives improved with the appetizers,
the truffled sauce, the capers in conch piccata,
with the ample portions on oversized plates,
the good wine, the sweet light in the clear glass lamp,
all reminding them of better times, of Paris,
of restaurants on the boulevard St. Germaine,
the Luxembourg Gardens, the lights on the Seine,
the honeymoon that continued on to Málaga.
"Remember that gypsy singer at El Figon?" he asked,
both of them now looking at the list of desserts,
"The one who called himself El Chocolaté?"

She smiled a wide Princess Grace of a smile.
And he, although not given to public displays,
took her hand and kissed it.

DESSERT

Chocolate Crunch Bar
with vanilla anglaise, strawberry sauce
and chocolate cigarette

Chocolate [*chocolatl,* from the Aztec *xocoatl*].
The Aztec royal drink chilled with mountain snow
frothed and spiced with honeyed cloves.
Montezuma drank it before going to his wives.
Cortés shipped it home in 1528. Now the couple
shares a plate, while sipping at their sherry,
remembering the song El Chocolaté sang:

> *When will the day come,*
> *that blissful morning when*
> *chocolate will be brought to us*
> *side by side in bed?*

Both of them now grateful, near the end of day,
for dinners that offer ease, like poetry or song.

Our generation has gradually learned the great art of living without security. We are prepared for anything . . . There is a mysterious pleasure in retaining one's reason and spiritual independence particularly in a period where confusion and madness are rampant.

STEFAN ZWEIG IN GEORGE PROCHNIK'S
THE IMPOSSIBLE EXILE

Romania, Romania

Looking at a map of Romania, one finds below Bîrlad, lost in the remote rolling hills near the crooked path of the Danube, not far from its Black Sea delta, the town of Bălăbănești, the "Place of the Balabans," chartered by Stefan the Great in 1520 after one of my ancestors rallied a peasant force that defeated "The Turk." Bălăbănești is a small farming town, just down the dusty road from the hamlet of Bălăbănye, both folded into the fields and hedgerows, along quiet streams forded by medieval, high-arched Turkish bridges.

Since the beginning of time, armies and marauders have swept through these fertile farmlands at the edge of Europe. Scythians, Thracians, Sarmatians. Names we hardly recognize. Empires, vanished overnight.

In AD 8, having annoyed Caesar Augustus, Ovid was banished to the Black Sea port of Tomis, now the Romanian city of Constanța. Ovid's *Tristia* and *Epistulae ex Ponto* are his last poems. Poems of an exile, aged, miserably separated from his family and following, relegated to a corner of the Pax Romana where Latin was not spoken, where literature was unknown. In his last works, he says he composed a poem in Getic, the local language. He says this with some embarrassment. Also, that one winter he stepped out with trepidation on the frozen Black Sea, and that he joined the citizenry at the ramparts to defend Tomis against barbarian horsemen who besieged the city with poison darts.

Hoc, ubi vivendum est, satis est, si consequor arvo . . . esse poeta. "Here, where I have to live, it will be enough to remain a poet."

Ovid, *Tristia* 5.10.15–22

Countless tribes roam about threatening savage war.
They think it disgraceful to live without plundering.
Outside, it's never safe. Our citadel defends itself
from weak ramparts, though strategically placed.
When the host descends, unexpected like birds,
We barely see them before they've seized their prey.
Often, gates shut, safe inside the walls,
we gather arrows fallen in the streets.

Innumerae circa gentes fera bella minantur,
        quae sibi non raptu vivere turpe putant.
Nil extra tutum est: tumulus defenditur ipse
        moenibus exiguis ingenioque loci.
Cum minime credas, ut aves, densissimus hostis
        advolat et praedam vix bene visus agit.
Saepe intra muros clausis venientia portis
        per medias legimus noxia tela vias.

The Siege

from the Romanian of Ştefan Augustin Doinaş

But when they went out of the city to surrender
they found the enemy nowhere to be seen.
POLYBIUS

The city at spear point. The army unseen.
Wells stopped, and smoke rising.
Our eagle standard, alive but not with valor,
we ate, without it sticking in our throats.
Then, the plagues. Ghosts from times past,
more faithful to their hearths than we, shot
arrows from ramparts, from far across the fields.
Nothing. Only a star-wound in a god's flesh.
Later, the clock of betrayal struck. Our drawbridge
fell from its pulleys. Cowards, faces to the earth,
begged forgiveness. But no one heard, only the moon
crossing the moat like the bow of a ship on the wind.
Yes, no one. Until the last of our deaths
we shall weep blood and suffer strangely,
doors open to evils, windows shattered.
Not a soul outside the city. But we, we surrendered.

Dr. Alice Magheru's Room

What a mess. The walls cluttered with paintings,
sketches, portraits. Photos: your father-in-law,
Prince Ghica of Samos, and his wife Alexandrina
who played piano with Liszt and Clara Schumann.
Carmen Silva, at her desk, pen in hand. A poem
she wrote for you in feathery blue ink.
The royal family posed beside a car.
A note from Queen Helene that calls you "dear."
Enescu and his nephew walking to a train.
A lithograph of General Magheru, muttonchopped

hero of the Turkish war, staring resolutely
across the Black Sea, hand on his sword hilt.
And books. Everywhere. Eight thousand books
piled on the floor, crammed into shelves, sliding
off desktops. Your husband's books of poetry,
his "antipoems" that had more vogue in France
and—leatherbound, titled in thin gold Roman type—
the medical texts you published together.
Bacteriologist, serologist, immunologist,
you made pills as the British bombed Bucharest.

East night you nap like a cat and read
while others sleep, stretching your eighty-seven
years into twice their human span. Last night
you spoke with your husband, dead for twenty years.
Today, you banter with a poet from America
whose taxi, when he leaves, rattles tram tracks
and cobblestones, halts at a light,
then nudges through crowds on Magheru Boulevard.

Earthquakes and armies have rolled down this street.
You've seen them come and go.

Like sound, the human spirit never dies
but fades, falters, filters off through space,
or is trapped in the laths of marble hearts.
In the quarries of the Parthenon
the shouts of masons murmur still,
caught in crystals like the quartz radio
I played with as a child. So it is, Alice,
with a soul sent out to others, signaling
from this room, this cell of powerful repose,
over the long years: the conscious mind.

Georgi Borisov in Paris

The Slavic poet sips his morning vodka, his mind
as troubled as the river sliding down below
the 22nd floor of his apartment on the Seine
where a barge cuts the surface to thread Pont Mirabeau.

He knows that words are fading from books.
From poems of Pushkin, from Apollinaire's,
from poems he wrote when talking in his dreams.
Words are disappearing, leaving pages bare.

Next door, an office complex bustles like a hive,
its workers tending cells inside the glassed-in combs.
He stares into their cubicles. It sours his vodka.
Their tower has become . . . a heap of drying bones.

But what can poets do about the missing words, gone
even from those lips that longed to say them—like wishes
floating off above the river, like coins
tossed from barges, bridges, *bateaux mouches*?

Where else is this happening? Is it happening at home?
In a world reduced to billboards, he would be totally unnerved.
The strangely exiled poet has been drinking for ten days
but this has only sharpened his worry about the words . . .

Let Him Be

translated, with Alexandra Veleva, from the Bulgarian
of Georgi Borisov

Let the man be who had nothing to tell you,
let him mumble his beard over his mug of gall,
let him work his bread into bits at the table.
Let him think he's coughing because the tobacco's damp.

And let him, as he leaves, nod goodbye to the bottle
and go outside and leap from the porch into the night
and stride across the fields already thick with clover
to wave down the first truck that finds him in its lights.

Let him tell the wicked driver all about his ulcer,
how it keeps him up, hungry at odd times,
and how bread is not enough, no, not by bread alone
despite whatever may be the common thought.

Let him get off at a hill and go up to a pear tree
and punch his fist right through the twisted trunk,
clean through to the night, and, as the tree listens,
let him curse it in pain and shame and bitter hurt.

Because, life picks us up like little chunks of rye bread
and wads and works us in its rough, sweaty fist.
So let him be, this man who's walking down the hillside.
Let him alone. Let him slam the table with his fist.

Ibn Fadhlan, the Arab Emissary,
Encounters Vikings on the Volga River, AD 922

The Rus, as they are called, camped above the river
trading furs from a log hall, axed out by slaves.
The men—tall as date palms, blond, tattooed—
had set a pole out front carved with gods
to which they offer things to bless their trade.
This was all I saw of their piety or conscience.
Caliph, they are the dirtiest creatures of God.

Each morning when the men stir out of sleep
a slave girl brings a bronze ablution bowl
first to the chief who washes his face, then
rinses his mouth, spits, and blows his nose
into the bowl which she carries around until
each has washed in the same filthy water.

When their lord died, a huge *sahirra dakhma*
(the witch who rules the slave girls) set them wailing
as they packed his corpse in black earth and
his men built a death ship with a funeral pyre.
They call this witch "Angel of Death," *Malak al-Mawt.*
She picked a girl to go with the dead lord, then
invited the men to fornicate with the slave girl
drugged and lost in a crazy song.

Then the girl was led to the ship
where the lord, his corpse now washed,
lay on the pyre wreathed in flowers and fruit.
Then the woman stabbed the girl
in her ribs as a man crept behind her

with a knotted rope, strangling her cries
until she fell dead and they laid her on the pyre.

Torching the ship, knocking away its blocks,
they shoved it blazing in the river, singing
their lord to a life of pleasures they imagine.
Soon his ship was ashes swirling on the currents.
O Caliph, through forested lands, west and north,
one finds only infidels with vile habits.
Some are Christian. Nothing will come of them.

Looking Out from the Acropolis, 1989

> *Each structure, in its beauty, was even then and at once antique, but*
> *in the freshness of its vigor, even today, recent and newly wrought.*
> PLUTARCH, ON THE ACROPOLIS

In old-town Athens of date palms, of ferned balconies
cascading canary calls, I walked with a Bulgarian friend
up the stony, sunny path to the "high city" where tangles
of cactus and Spanish sword pocked the Periclean ramparts
and packs of wild cats prowled the brush for mice as wind
whipped the naps of their fur and Georgi's little son, Aleko,
hooted after them as we trailed behind, plodding upward
through the gate of broken columns to the precincts of Athena,
two poets, from West and East, here for the first time, awed
by the lonely grace of stones fallen, stones still standing.

On the left, the smiling maidens of the caryatid porch
whose marble robes fluttered in blue sky;
on the right, the massive surge of Parthenon columns
capped by a parade of centaurs, horsemen, gods,
reliving dramas of who we are, who we might become
as pediments marked our battles with beasts, our talks
with gods, our search for ourselves in philosopher groves
of this city on the hill that draws us by surviving
Persian navies, Roman consuls, pasha's yoke, *Panzergruppe*
—holding up like a Phidean model a sense
of the examined life that is worth living, a place
where gods and men can struggle with success, striving
to widen the wealth of the human soul, the size of heaven.
All across the monumental rubble, trailing after tour guides,
Japanese photographed this field of broken stone.

As we looked out from the Acropolis, we saw
the New World Order the President praised
that winter as caged canaries down below
sang in the sunshine of Athenian balconies:
Both superpowers, bankrupt; the Japanese, our bankers.
Looking east past Yugoslavian slaughter,
the Kozlodui reactor was about to blow.
Farther east, in Tbilisi, the shoot-out at Parliament,
the breadlines in Moscow, the dead rivers and lakes,
the black colonels hopping in Rumpelstiltskin rage
at loss of empire, as Chechens, Kurds, Azeris et al.
went for their guns to settle old scores.
How much has changed since then?
Merely the killing fields.

Then it was Israeli rubber bullets and intifada stones.
Holiday shoppers at Clapham Junction bombed by Irish Santas.
German skinheads bashing Vietnamese and Turks.
Bloated African bellies, fly-infested eyes.
Shining Path Maoists beheading Indians in Ayacucho.
And nosferatu warlords in Beijing sipping their elixir
of cinnabar and blood. Pol Pot vacationing in Thailand.

Meanwhile, it was snowing in Chicago, snowing on the cardboard huts
of the homeless in the land of the free, as more banks failed
and repossessed Midwestern farms lay fallow to the wind.
Each in the cell of himself was almost convinced of his freedom
when the Wall fell to cheers of freed multitudes
and one could hear communist and capitalist gasps rise up
in a global shout that circled the earth for a year
then disappeared through holes in the ozone layer.

— • —

The New World Order. The tribes of the Book
are still turned to wrath as the worst of us
would wind time back to savage pasts easier to imagine.
The philosopher's grove is empty; the poet's words gone flat.
Against this, aren't the Japanese, baptized in nuclear fire,
clapping their hands for the Kami of the cash register,
our safest, sanest neighbors?

— • —

These old stones cry out for more.
Surviving centuries, sculpted for all to see,
declaring our need for beauty and laws like love
for this tiny *polis* of a planet spinning wildly,
for my daughter, snug, asleep in her bed,
for Aleko who played in the Chernobyl cloud,
whose father stood near Nike's rotting frieze,
looking out upon the city jammed with cars. Georgi
opened his flask of vodka and poured some on a stone
before we drank our toasts to the new world order
and to whatever muse might come to give us words.

A Finger

After most of the bodies were hauled away
and while the FBI and Fire Department and NYPD
were still haggling about who was in charge, as smoke cleared,
the figures in Tyvek suits came, gloved, gowned, masked,
ghostly figures searching rubble for pieces of people,
bagging, then sending the separate and commingled remains
to the temporary morgue set up on site.
This is where the snip of forefinger began its journey.

Not alone, of course, but with thousands of other bits not lost
or barged off with the tonnage for sorting at the city landfill.
A delicate tip, burnt and marked "finger, distal" and sent over
to the Medical Examiner's, where forensic anthropologists
sorted human from animal bones from Trade Center restaurants,
all buried together in the Pompeian effect of incinerated dust.

The bit of finger (that might have once tapped text messages,
potted a geranium, held a glass, stroked a cat, tugged
a kite string along a beach) went to the Bio Lab
where it was profiled, bar-coded, and shelved in a Falcon tube.
Memorial Park—that is to say: the parking lot behind the ME—
droned with generators for the dozens of refrigerated trucks
filling with human debris, while over on the Hudson at Pier 94
families brought toothbrushes or lined up for DNA swabbing.

As the year passed, the unidentified remains were dried out
in a desiccation room—humidity pumped out, heat raised high—
shriveled, then vacuum sealed.

                                But the finger tip had
a DNA match in a swab from her brother. She was English.

Thirty years old. She worked on the 105th floor of the North Tower.
The *Times* ran a bio. Friends posted blogs. Her father
will not speak about it. Her mother planted a garden in Manhattan.
In that garden is a tree. Some look on it and feel restored.
Others, when the wind lifts its leaves, want to scream.

After the Inauguration, 2013

Without the shedding of blood, there is no remission of sins.
EPISTLE TO THE HEBREWS, 9:22

Pulling from the tunnel at Union Station, our train
shunts past DC offices and then crosses the rail bridge
over the tidal Potomac blooming in sweeps of sunlight.
Except for me and two young guys in suits studying
spreadsheets on their laptops, and the tattooed girl
curled asleep across two seats, and the coiffed blonde lady
confined to her wheelchair up front next to piled luggage,
it's mostly Black folk, some trickling home in high spirits,
bits of Inaugural bunting and patriotic ribbons
swaying from their suitcase handles on the overhead racks,
all of us riding the *Carolinian* south.

Farther on, where it's suddenly sailboats and gulls
on a nook of the Chesapeake, the banked-up railbed
cuts through miles of swamped pines and cypress
as the train trundles past the odd heron stalking frogs,
or, picking up speed, clatters through open cornfields
where, for a few seconds, staring through the dirty glass,
you can spot turkeys scrabbling the stubble. Farther south,
past Richmond, something like snow or frost glints off a field
and you realize it's just been gleaned of cotton
and this is indeed the South. As if to confirm this fact
to all of us on Amtrak, some latter-day Confederate
has raised the rebel battle flag in a field of winter wheat.

At dusk, just outside Raleigh, the train slows
and whistles three sharp calls at crossing in Kittrell, NC.
Along the railroad tracks, under dark cedars, lie graves
of Confederates from Petersburg's nine-month siege, men

who survived neither battle, nor makeshift hospital
at the Kittrell Springs Hotel, long gone from the town
where our train now pauses for something up ahead.
Nearby in Oxford, in 1970, a Black GI was shot to death.
One of his killers testified: "That nigger committed suicide,
coming in here wanting to four-letter-word my daughter-in-law."
Black vets, just back from Vietnam, set the town on fire.
Off in the night, you could see the flames from these rails
that once freighted cotton, slaves, and armies.

                                                  Now our Amtrak
speeds by, passengers chatting, or snoozing, or just looking out
as we flick on past the shut-down mills, shotgun shacks, collapsed
tobacco barns, and the evening fields with their white chapels
where "The Blood Done Sign My Name" is still sung, where
the past hovers like smoke or a train whistle's call.

Gods and Empire

1. XENOPHANES FLEES BEFORE THE PERSIANS

If horses and oxen had hands and could draw pictures,
their gods would look remarkably like horses and oxen.
XENOPHANES OF COLOPHON, 570–480 BCE

All day we trudged north along the Aegean, cold rain
squalling, whipping up whitecaps, churning sandbars,
eating the beach, rocking pines, hissing sand-sleet.

But the hardest storms came at night, scouring us
huddled in dunes as strikes of violet light flashed
off the cliffs, igniting our faces when thunder boomed

and we, caught out not by pursuers, but by *the gods*
the soldiers whined, as they crouched under leather shields,
like dogs in the deafening downpour. By morning,

the sea was calm and we saw the sun and moon
together. So close they almost touched. The shoreline
was now rain-rinsed, wind-brushed, smoothed,

and all about strewn with the crania of huge jellyfish
fading like lanterns in the sunlit air, under a rainbow,
dying like gods in throes of contemplation, or so I jested,

a philosopher fleeing with soldiers, perplexing them
with "She whom you call Iris, or rainbow, is merely cloud.
Sing a dirge for her," I said, "if you think she is divine,"

adding we were weakened by superstition and by luxury
like the Lydians oblivious to threat, idling about in purple robes,
boastful, comely, proud, each anointed with rich perfumes.

Soon we heard trumpets drifting off the headlands.
Soon we saw the Medes' war chariots, their sacrificial knives, heard
their prophets screaming. Saw their crudely fashioned gods.

2. XENOPHANES IN EXILE IN GREECE AND SICILY

*The following are fit topics for conversation for men reclining
on a soft couch by the fire in the winter season, . . . Who are you,
and what is your family? Where is your land, my friend?
How old were you when the Medes invaded your land?*

FRAGMENTS OF XENOPHANES

What does it matter if the women
of Colophon are no longer given
to stroll the streets in flowing, sea-purple robes?

That the pipe no longer leads seductive odes
sung in the voluptuous Lydian modes?
That Medes now temper their swords on our hearths?

Walking on Colophon's foggy shore at night
I once was the center of a circle of sight.
The wheel of a chariot has one locus.

My eye circumscribed the radius of the real.
Behind me the fog cloaked what it revealed
while before me it opened like the folds of a robe.

Strained with a vision, my self began to breathe.
At twenty my poems were known across the sea
and then we heard the trumpets of the Asian tribes.

Now I am an amusement to strangers, drinking
their wine at banquets. For sixty-seven years thinking
my thoughts, while tossed restlessly up and down Greece.

Such is Xenophanes, aged *rhapsode* and lover of wisdom,
who looked into all things of earth and heaven
and made of them a song, sung in a time of barbarians.

Poetry Reading by the Black Sea

Often, gates shut, safe inside the walls,
we gathered arrows fallen in the streets.

OVID, *TRISTIA* 5.10.21–22

A breeze riffles in from the beach
stirring poplar catkins, woolly stuff
drifting the town in flurries, searching

the air like syllables of poetry while
we perch on the stones of this Roman bath
listening to poetry, the delicate thing which lasts.

Here at empire's edge, boys, silly with love,
chatted idly by the pools. Merchants,
trading amphoras of oil and Lydian dye,

cursed thin profits, cruel seas, lost ships.
Now seagulls flap and squawk on broken walls
scurfed with weeds and the royal poppy.

Greek and Roman, Getae, Thracian, Bulgar,
Slavs, Avars, Goths, Celts, Tatars, Huns,
Arabs, Turks, Russians, and, now, the US Navy.

Not far from here, one frigid winter in Tomis,
an aging Ovid, exiled by Augustus,
donned a helmet to defend the ramparts

as Thracian horsemen circled the frozen marsh,
their long hair tinkling with chinks of ice,
shooting poisoned arrows into the walled city

killing the boy who attended the old poet,
the boy he paid to massage his skin, there
in "the last place," among barbarians

two thousand years ago. And, now, acacias
fragrance our evening as poplar fluff floats by
over imperial rubble. "Only poetry lasts."

"The smell of autumn rain ..."

from the Romanian of Benjamin Fundoianu
Herța, 1917

The smell of autumn rain and hay hung
about the village, soaking the lungs.
Girls dawdled on the dirty streets
which filled with silence each evening.
The postman shuffled by, slow, hooded, deaf.
Hay wagons—chased by rain—had left
and silence settled and grew moldy as
simple folk whispered Yiddish in their homes.
The drizzle snuffed a gaslight with a hiss,
hissed back by geese waddling to a house.
Leaves were rotting in the old bell's mouth.
We heard these awkward autumn sounds:
the mailcoach rattling in from Dorohoi,
the oxen rising from the bare soil,
bellowing, heads back as if to suck the sky.
The village bellowed back with reddish eyes.

Benjamin Fondane was a poet and philosopher, born Benjamin Wechsler in Iași, Romania, in 1898. He was the son of Isac Wechsler, a small tradesman from Herța (in Bucovina), and Adela, sister of Jewish scholars Elias Wilhelm and Moses Schwarzfeld. In Romania, before taking off for Paris and avant-garde renown, he wrote under the name of Fundoianu.

Herța

by Benjamin Fundoianu

În tîrg miroase-a ploaie, a toamna și a fîn.
Vîntul nisip aduce, fierbinte, în plămîn,
și fetele așteaptă în ulița murdară
tăcerea care cade în fiecare seară,
și factorul, cu gluga pe cap, greoi și surd.
Căruțe fugărite de ploaie au trecut,
și liniștea în lucruri demult mucegăiește.
În case oameni simpli vorbesc pe ovreiește.
Gîște, cu pantofi galbeni, vin lent, după-un zaplaz;
auzi cum ploaia stinge fanarele cu gaz,
cum învechește frunza în clopote de-aramă -
auzi tăcerea lungă și gri care e toamnă
și diligenta care vine din Dorohoi.
Pustiu, din șes, se urcă cirezile de boi,
și cum mugesc, cu capul întors, de parc-ar suge -
cu ochii roșii, tîrgul, cuprins de spaimă, muge.

Préface en Prose

from the French of Benjamin Fundoianu
translated with Donka Farkas

I am talking to you, my opposite Others.
I am talking man to man
with that bit of myself which remains a man,
that bit of my voice still stuck in my throat.
My blood is on the streets, may it—oh, may it not—
cry out for vengeance.
The hunter's horn is sounded. The hounds are on the track.
So let me now speak to you in words we once shared
though few still make sense.

A day will come, for sure, when thirst quenched,
we will have gone beyond memory, and death
will have finished hatred's work, and I
will have become a bunch of nettles under your feet.
But, look, you need to know I had a face like you.
A mouth that prayed, like you.

When a speck of dust or a dream
entered my eyes, they wept a little salt.
And when a nasty thorn pricked my skin
it bled red blood, just like yours.
And, yeah, like you, I was cruel, and hungered
for tenderness, for power, money, pleasure, and pain.
Just like you I was mean, filled with anguish,
reliable enough at peace, drunk in victory,
and staggering and worn in times of failure.

And, sure, I was a man like other men
nourished by bread, by dreams, and by despair,

and sure, I loved, wept, hated, and suffered.
I bought flowers and sometimes I skipped on my rent.
On Sundays, I might go to the countryside and fish,
to catch, under God's eye, his fish of irreality
and bathe in the river that sang in the bulrushes
and eat fries in the evening. Later, I'd go back
and sleep, my heart worn out and lonely,
full of pity for myself, full of pity for mankind,
searching, searching in vain on a woman's body
for that impossible peace we lost once in a great orchard
with the tree of life flowering at its heart.

Like you I read all the newspapers, the books,
and understood nothing of the world,
understood nothing about men,
though often I may have claimed to.
When death, when death came, perhaps
I pretended to understand but, really,
(I can tell you now)
when all of death entered my astonished eyes
I was stunned by how little I had understood.
Did you understand it any better?

And, yet . . . *no!*
I wasn't a man like you.
You were not born on the road.
No one ever dropped your children into a sewer
like blind kittens, you never had to wander
from city to city, tracked by cops.
You never knew calamity at dawn,
or cattle cars, or bitter sobs of humiliation
when accused of a crime you never committed,
a murder without a body, or had to change your name
and face, not to have an abused name or a face that served
as a spittoon.

But a day will come, for sure, when this poem
will lie before you, asking nothing.
Leave it. Leave it. It's just an outcry.
You can't turn that into a poem.
(Will I have time to polish this?)
But when you tread on this clutch of nettles
that was once me, reading this in some other century
like an outdated story, remember that I was innocent
and that like you, mortals of your day, I too
had a face marked by anger, and by pity, and by joy.

A man's face, quite simply.

This poem, probably Fundoianu's last, was written in 1944, the year the Nazis took him
and his sister first to Drancy and then to Auschwitz, where they perished.

The Alibi

from the Romanian of Ştefan Augustin Doinaş

*We can't do anything in this world without risking
the deaths of others.*

ALBERT CAMUS, *THE PLAGUE*

Endlessly, on the fields, in archways,
on the street, in woods, on altars, in bed,
day and night, someone commits murder.

Was I present? The bulging eye
clouds over and shuts. The hand denies
it was an accomplice.

Was I there?
A blotch of blood upon the brow
is passed from father to son.

I saw the stab and the collapse.
I heard the cry. And then
the knife, dripping, blinded me.

But I saw him. I know he is among us,
but I cannot say his name. What name
will fit all the many children,

sick on games and jokes,
who murder their childhood?
Lovers enter the thigh

of the madman, and die in quicklime.
A flock of crows wheels
about their bodies. And all is hopeless.

What flag shall we fly over the city?
Where shall we flee? All roads are cut.
Like God Who Is Everywhere,

we had a hand in all these deaths.
Accomplices—yet whose? Stuff my mouth
with rags so I can't speak.

The unborn of our honored race
sleep soundly. They have an alibi.

Returning after Our War

But in Indochina I drained a magic potion, a loving cup
which I have shared since with many retired colons *and officers*
of the Foreign Legion, whose eyes light up at the mention
of Saigon and Hanoi.

GRAHAM GREENE, *WAYS OF ESCAPE*

I. SAIGON

The other night, I went with friends to see the Saigon River where it loops
past the venerable Majestic Hotel, still standing on the riverbank at the end
of the modernized, old downtown. From the hotel's top-floor balcony, we
looked across to the Nhà Bè side from where, back in the American days, rock-
ets were sometimes launched at the city from the mangrove swamps across the
way. We stood awhile saying nothing, just watching the boats chugging slowly
behind dim bow lights as a full moon floated above the river.

During the war, the street behind the Majestic was—architecturally speak-
ing—still a colonial avenue of small shops, GI bars, cafés, Maxim's nightclub
(still there), and green-shuttered *appartements* with yellow stuccoed walls
leaking blotches of mildew.

Now it's a dazzle of luxury hotels and skyscrapers. Downtown Saigon is nearly
unrecognizable but, every now and then, my taxi would turn a corner, stirring
up a memory of some distant encounter . . . an argument in a government
ministry, a flower market where I once bought a pair of finches, or simply our
corner cigarette stall where a gold-toothed old lady sold Marlboros tapped up
with marijuana.

Behind the Majestic, the old Graham Greene apartment is gone, though one
remembers the man who prepared Greene's opium, still climbing the creaky
wooden steps into the early '70s to serve Americans with his valise of pipes.
Now, after many re-inventions, it's become a garish complex of glass and metal
called "Katina" as the global imperium changed hands over the decades and

the Rue Catinat became Tu Do or Freedom Street, and then, after our war, Đồng Khởi, or Great Uprising, and Saigon became Ho Chi Minh City.

2. THE OPIUM PILLOW

> *That night I woke from one of those short deep opium sleeps, ten minutes long, that seem a whole night's rest . . .*
> GRAHAM GREENE, *THE QUIET AMERICAN*

A cool ceramic block, a brick
just larger than one's cheek,

cream-colored, bordered in blue,
a finely crackled glaze, but smooth,

a hollow bolster on which to lay
one's head before it disappears

in curls of acrid opium fumes
slowly turning in the tropical room

lit by a lampwick's resinous light
snaking shadows up a wall.

The man who served us with his pipes,
with tarred and practiced hands,

worked a heated wad of rosin
"cooked the color of a cockroach wing"

into the pinhole of the fat pipe bowl.
He said, "Draw." One long pull

that drew in combers of smoke rolling
down the lungs like the South China Sea,

crashing on the mind's frail shell
that rattled, then wallowed, and filled with sand.

—◦—

I woke up to animal groans . . .
Down in the stairwell Flynn and Stone

were beating up a young thief
who had broken in to steal their bikes

bucking an M16 against the kid's ear
then punching him in the stomach with its butt

before they bum-rushed him out the door
doubled over, and wheezing for air.

I stammered *no* in a syllable that rose
like a bubble lifting off the ocean floor.

Ten days later, they were dead. Flynn
and Stone, who dealt in clarities of force,

who motorcycled out to report the war,
shot at a roadblock on Highway One.

Nearly all those Saigon friends are gone now.
Gone like smoke. Like incense.

for Tom and John Steinbeck, Crystal Eastin Erhart Steinbeck Brown,
Steve Erhart, Sean Flynn, and Louise and Dana Stone, all gone

3. ABANDONED HOUSE, SAIGON

Two swallows fly in a broken window, sweeping under
yellow orchids tumbling from the rotted frame.

The ghost up there has stopped her complaining
while out in the rain below a tarp, a girl selling soup

squats by the curb slicing tiny hoops of chili,
piling little heaps of red on a white dish.

Did the ghost upstairs learn English or French?
Where did she intend to go? Why does she linger?

How her lips must burn when her fingers brush them.
One swallow darts out the darkened window

while over in LA, stuck in traffic, a Vietnamese guy
remembers this street, the vendor, the house lying almost empty.

Goodbye to the Lake

sleeping in the heart of Hanoi
where the elderly gather at dawn
for tai chi, windmilling their arms
and chatting as they walk the lakeside paths.

Goodbye to the feathery Hoàng Điệp trees
leaning over the water toward the little island
with its shrine for the ancient hero
who gave back the sacred sword.

And goodbye to the old woman
sitting zazen every morning by the water's edge
as the lake watches her with its glassine
sentient eye, and sometimes blinks.

Once we had been so close we shared each other's dreams

———————————————

For John Steinbeck IV (1947–1991)

I used to dread his calls, yanking me out of sleep
for decades after Vietnam, his drunken talk,
his deep insistence growling through the phone,
his irritation with my sleep, my middle-class retreat.
Once we had been so close we shared each other's dreams

carousing in Saigon, and later, London, stoned by memories
of the war, of R&R with the Mekong river monks
who offered puzzled welcomes to the pals he dubbed
"lysergic Buddhists," visiting Phoenix Island, where
he played a bamboo flute and talked of famous priests

from the line of jungle prophets schooled in crazy song:
the Master of the Western Peace, the Monk Who Sells Potatoes,
the Coconut Monk, breathing the Perfume from Precious Mountain,
all dharma teachers whose unlettered lives erased his father's fame.
He knew I knew the pain he carried with his name.

His last call came on Tet the year before he died,
dialed from the East LA pagoda he conned to take him in.
Dead broke except for his expensive name, he complained
its abbot kept scolding him for drinking, said he smelled.
What would the spirits say in their heavenly report?

Indeed, what will they say in the Heavenly Report?
He played a bamboo flute and talked of Buddhist priests.
That some friends knew the pain he carried with his name
and that he visits time to time and tries to stir their dreams
with flutesong and scents . . . drifting off Precious Mountain.

At Nora's House, Shepard's Roost, Atlantic Beach, NC, Where I Wrote Many of My Poems

Out beyond the porthole above the kitchen sink
a line of pelicans skims a breaker, wing tips

brushing the tattering crest as if to feel the herring
running inside the green lung of the recoiling wave

scales flashing as the school flips a turn and the roller
rises then collapses along this south-facing beach.

All morning, terns plunging up plumes of sea-spray
have been flying off with mullet wriggling in their bills.

Last night, as dials of dune grass marked time in the sand
and while the summer's clock of stars circled the Pole

a fox curled in a hollow, snug in the sea-oat dunes.
A huge green turtle struggled ashore to nest.

In the house's cool cellar, Shep's rowboat—dry-docked
and drifting with the years—still trails a wake of sunlight

and salt marsh, crab pots, duck blinds, bay chop
slapping boat chines, and Nora and the girls, laughing.

Tide Pool

Nature is at times a shameless playwright.
JOHN BARTH

Here the ancient lava slid into the sea,
hissed up steam clouds, then cooled into stone

making a moonscape in the volcanic shelf
pocked with basins, cracked by runnels

where tides chafe canyons day and night
scooping out clear shallow pools,

sand-bottomed cisterns, where sun shaft
and tide-froth ply their metaphors.

At the pool's edge, a hermit crab with ivory claw,
pop-dot blue eyes, and strawberry whiskers

sidles off under some dead shell.
In the tidal rinse, blue neon fingerlings

flit between the rocks. Fiddlers swim away
at the shift of a shadow and deeper down

beneath wrinkles of light in the tide-washed crooks
the ink-purple urchins wait for whatever.

A sun and a moon, but a fishbowl nonetheless
for little lives in their amorous wriggles,

for the crashing sea punching holes below the shelf
flushing innocent worlds, leaving only

a stone stage for watery dramas beneath the sky,
an existential entertainment, an opera mimicking

our desire for an imagined home, in a place
forever perishing, a place to live.

Waiting for the Painter to Return

for Susan Jane Adams, 1944–2012

All the trees were drinking from the fog
spilling over hillsides—the pines, and

farther down, an apple orchard, gnarled
and abandoned. Along the creek

the acacias flushed yellow, as gophers
gnawed around under the old pasture.

Her jasmine continued to climb the porch
and seemed willing to consider spring.

Above the barn studio, its tin roof was quieted
by the fog, and listening as her paintings

offered each other their critiques, everything
waiting for the gate to open, her car to pull in.

Remembering Elling Eide (1935–2012)

Sent to Tu Fu
from beneath the city wall at Sandhill

Why have I come here after all?
To rest in retreat by the Sandhill wall.
By the side of the wall are some ancient trees
with the sounds of autumn both night and day.
But I can't get drunk on the wines of Lu,
and my feelings are wasted in the songs of Ch'i.
My thoughts of you like the River Wen
go rolling southward endlessly.
ELLING EIDE'S TRANSLATION FROM
THE CHINESE OF LI PO

Around dawn the hurricane died and neighbors crept out to see
their snapped trees, lawns littered with leaf mash and roof bits
blown into heaps with siding, broken birds, and snakes.

By afternoon, chainsaws were screaming
in the sickening August heat and bulldozers began
to scrape the rotting tonnage from the streets.

That's when Elling drove over from Sarasota
in his old VW van packed with candles, with
dog food, cat food, flashlights and batteries,

jugs of water, a frozen cake dripping icing, crackers,
caviar, a chilled case of Tsingtao beer, chainsaw blades,
and tropical trees to plant the place again.

In a few years, our new ylang-ylang rose
thirty feet, unfurling long yellow blossoms
to fill our evenings with attar of Chanel.

And so it went with Elling's palms,
his gumbo-limbo, Cuban guanabana,
papaya, bananas, and bamboo, the house

again shaded, overhung with bougainvillea,
trellised in passion vine, scented by gardenia,
by Burmese orchids that drink the humid air.

Once again, parrots flock the sea grape for its fruit,
the "birds assembling as if to audit the Dharma"
as Elling once translated Li Po's lines. And now,

like the Taoist poet, Elling has gone off somewhere
and our thoughts for him "like the River Wen
go rolling southward endlessly."

Showgirl

for Tally Richards (1928–2008)

Like Mary of Egypt, her patron saint,
she roamed the desert and her travels weren't easy,
getting to Taos by way of The Sands and The Copacabana
after running off from the chorus line in Vegas
with $400 in her hip pocket. Before her escape
she watched an A-Bomb blast out in the desert
with Jimmy Durante who liked to call her Richard.

She said
she loved the revues, her rhinestones and ostrich plumes.
Nevermind the night she got tipsy and mocked a mobster
who followed her to her hotel room with a tire iron,
shoved her on the bed, and pressed the greasy metal
against her perfect face.

Oh, such a long way from the Catfish and Pee Dee rivers
and the small Georgia town where her father ran a store and
where, boy crazy at 15 and hot to trot, she ran off with an older kid
and was married for a few weeks
until it was annulled.

Years later, in Taos, she'd sit with her cigarettes in the cool dark
of her adobe art gallery and joke about the men she liked,
their mayhem and punch-ups, the painter who shot a guy
in the nuts for coming on to his son, her aging Greek boyfriend
who owned the hotel on the plaza where he lived with his mother,
the antics of actors, writers, and provocateurs. The painters
whose early work she showed until they got famous or dead.

Little explains her eye for art,
or her elegant prose in *Art in America,* or her fierce
enigmatic feuds, the rubble of her romances, her
melancholy life alone
with Pinky, her dyspeptic cat painted by Fritz Scholder, or
her languorous voice drifting like smoke,
like mist through Georgia pines.

Three Men Dancing on a River Shore

Qing Dynasty Serving Platter, Blue-and-White Porcelain

In the background, you can see the city they left behind
when they crossed the river to dance on this shore,
three gentlemen in mandarin robes and scruffy beards
now jigging on the sand under pines and willows
accompanied by musicians on trumpet, flute, and drum
and one plying a squeeze-box of some kind
for these scholars waving their hands above their heads,
kicking up sand and celebrating friendship, their dharma bridge
for getting to the other side, however briefly.

Three men dancing. Not drunk, just immensely amused
knowing that soon enough there would be only the wind
shushing its sad music along an empty shore.

for Tim Buckley and Tracy McCallum

In the desert there is nothing but the presence of Allah

ARAB PROVERB

Cibolero

During this time Castillo saw, on the neck of an Indian, a little buckle
from a sword-belt, and in it was sewed a horseshoe nail. He took it from
the Indian, and we asked what it was; they said it had come from Heaven.
We further asked who had brought it, and they answered that some men,
with beards like ours, had come from Heaven to that river; that
they had horses, lances and swords, and had lanced two of them.

THE JOURNEY OF ALVAR NUÑEZ CABEZA DE VACA (1542)
TRANSLATED BY FANNY BANDELIER (1905)

It's 7:00 a.m. in Tecolote, New Mexico,
and the local news on cable
is going on about some woman high on dust
crashing into kids at a crossing. Meanwhile,
out on the edge of the high prairie,
up by I-25, the inmates are rising off
their roosts at San Miguel county jail
where the jail log reads like catechism:

> Criminal Sexual Penetration in the first degree. Assault with the intent
> to commit violent felony. False imprisonment. Extortion. Unlawful
> taking of a motor vehicle. Conspiracy. Burglary of a structure. Con-
> tributing to the delinquency of a minor. Kidnapping. Conspiracy to
> commit Aggravated Battery. Aggravated DWI (7th offense). Posses-
> sion of drug paraphernalia. Driving on suspended revoked license.
> Probation Violation: Possession of marijuana, Possession of Meth-
> amphetamine. Aggravated stalking. Aggravated battery on household
> member, resisting, evading, violation of a restraining order, obstruct-
> ing an officer. Vehicular Homicide, Aggravated DUI, Open Con-
> tainer, Reckless driving. Assault with a deadly weapon. Assault with
> intent to commit a violent felony, with intent to commit mayhem.

The key word here is "mayhem," spreading through
the internet airwaves across the vast Llano Estacado

where mountains break into mesas and scrub,
dotted with piñon, cut by arroyos and twisty creeks
and a web of old footpaths made by ancestors.
And where the internet's thousand channels
are offering their social contracts, so
whether you are watching from prison, or at home
in your double-wide, or in the sleep cab of your semi,
or in your townhouse at the city's edge, or at Urgent Care,
the local laundromat, or in a bar that never closes,
wherever you are watching, you are probably just sitting
(and doing this a lot) tuned to hucksters selling
vacuum cleaners and Jesus, channel by channel:
#9012: Puppy Pooping in the House?
#9013: Thick Hair Guaranteed
#9014: Rev. Run's Sunday Suppers
#9015: Suffer from Lower Back Pain?
Mayhem being confusion turned to violence or lassitude.

But whether in the lockup looking out,
or among the hardworking folk of the Llano
in adobe-and-stone compounds and corrals
in, say, Ojitos Frios, Tecolote, or Villanueva,
when they see the rain dropping its dark curtains
over the vast plain, some Spenglerian twinge of memory
must arrive . . . of the massive adobe pueblo at Pecos,
of Vázquez de Coronado with his armored men on horses,
or, later, as the centuries stood still and Spanish dreams collapsed,
of trading with Comanches and learning to hunt buffalo
charging bareback into the stampeding herd with lowered lance,
shoving it into a thundering beast until it stumbled and crashed down
with all its wealth of meat, tallow, bone, and hide. A barrel
of buffalo tongues for the Viceroy in Mexico. *Cibolero,*
Buffalo Hunter. From *cíbola,* Spanish for "bison," from Zuni, *tzibola.*
Cíbola, the city of gold that was never found.

Coyote past Sunset

Finally, after a whole day of tailing trucks,
the highways loud with tire whine and bumper glare,
he got onto a blacktop running south to Mexico,
just him on the road, and off in the desert, dust devils
swirling over greasewood and yucca spikes,
ruffling the vultures sunning on fence posts
and whipping up grit around the odd horse
or pronghorns grazing with cattle, as he sped on
past hundreds of miles of barbed-wire fences.

After dusk, when he was nearly there, the moon
rose over the Chinati Mountains lighting cottonwoods
as he crossed the dry arroyo at the town limits.
Everything felt good, he thought. It was good to be alone.
That's when he saw the coyote trotting the berm,
turning its head to give him a haggard look, licking the air,
then padding out toward the high desert, past a house
with its TV flickering, the family at its meal.

El Mercado

You know on walking in, seeing
the big display of flyswatters
next to the dusty ketchup bottles,
the aisle of chips and salsa, the corn dogs,
the radishes aging in their bins,
the rotting avocados

. . . know that few pass through here, that few
stop in this high desert town by the border,
and that whatever you've come looking for
you probably won't find.

El Cementerio de la Merced

The likeness of the heart is that of a feather blown about by the wind in the desert.

ABU MUSA AL-ASH'ARI, VOL. 1, BOOK 1, HADITH 88

Some pronghorn antelope have gotten through the barbed-wire fence
and into the graveyard, looking for shade in the cedars and pines,

or perhaps just fooled by the plastic flowers, and now are grazing
among the Spanish headstones and pointed, wooden crosses,

lifting and dropping their horned heads, their parched white faces,
as they amble by a gravelly plot for three women, buried together:

Elizabeth, Dolores, and Addie, the last to go, at 80, in 2002.
Why do they share a gravesite, with their stones inscribed in English?

Why aren't they in the Anglo graveyard across the fence?
Back in town, I asked some older women but no one knew them.

So, who buried them? No such names are in the local phone book.
Nor on the graves nearby, here in the ghostly Texan *despoblado.*

Looking for the lights

around midnight, his pickup shut off, engine still ticking,
parked off a road running through ancient lava flows

dotted with mesquite and ocotillo, with cactus and yucca,
he listened to a javelina pack snuffling nearby in a dry wash

in the cool dry night air pulling up from Pinto Canyon,
from the Chinati Mountains just above the border,

not a ranch house light for miles, just Orion stalking a full moon,
as he leaned against his dusty tailgate looking for the Light,

that is, the Marfa Lights that wink above the desert brush,
the Lights that local Indians took for star people visiting Earth,

and early ranchers tried to ride down, thinking them campfires
of Mexican or Apache rustlers from across the Rio Grande.

— • —

When he first heard it barreling down the blacktop, lights flashing,
he figured it for an ambulance speeding to rescue some rancher

but after it pulled to a screeching halt and wheeled its headlights on him,
roof-rack lights strobing blue-and-red across the road and berm, and

a voice called from behind the driver's opened door, and then the spotlight
flicked on, blinding him, he knew it was the Border Patrol and, most likely,

there was a gun on him as well. He explained he was an American
and that he was here looking for the Lights. "The what?"

"The Marfa Lights," he said. They had a nice talk after that, but
across the roadway in the night. So he never actually *saw* the agent,

who said he had never seen the Lights himself but knew people who had,
before driving off, leaving him to desert prairie and streams of stars.

Back then

looking for some peace of mind
was like searching for a cricket in a field.
He'd head out, following his best directions
only to drive around from noon to nightfall
past bogs and cornfields and tangly woods.
His car would get stuck, or the battery die
and he would have to hump it to a farmhouse to call for a tow.
Back in town, he would sit at the bar with a beer,
wondering why the locals were lying,
and slapping mosquitoes whining at his ear.
He had all the right gear, just couldn't get there.

One evening he spotted a mule deer
ambling up a hillside path
and he followed it to higher ground
as a huge moon rose off the ridge
and he caught the scent of pine needles.
So he kept on until dark, reaching a ledge
overlooking Phantom Lake and the ghost town.
His breath fogged in the cooling mountain air.
Moonlight seemed to pour from his nostrils.
He made camp there, sleeping that night
in a mess of dreams, troubled with bat squeaks,
with wild burros braying along the nearby creek.

At dawn the bats were pocketed upside down
in hollows of the canyon wall rinsing in pink light
and he saw the burros grazing wheatgrass and sage.
At the canyon head, a cave yawned open
but empty of the voices that muttered in the night.
And the blasted tree, high on the mesa rim

—that writhed at dusk like a man crucified—
was a tree again, rocking in the wind.
Stars gone, the sky streaked in sunlight.
A canyon wren, perched in a willow,
plied the dawn with inquiring song.

The Writing Life

Somewhere, sometime, in many travels and moves, I acquired a copy of William Hogarth's print *The Distrest Poet* (ca. 1736), depicting a poet sitting at his desk in cramped quarters beneath a slanted attic window as he looks off distractedly, holding his quill pen in one hand and scratching his bewigged head with the other. A mop and bucket are near his feet, next to his chevalier's sword lying on the bare floorboards. A baby is asleep on a bed behind him. His wife sits in a chair nearby, sewing a pair of trousers, cat at her feet, and behind her some clothes are drying on the screen before the fireplace. Their door is open and a woman is standing in it talking with the poet's wife. A little dog gnaws at something left on a plate on a chair. Above the chair, fixed to the wall, is an open and empty wooden bread box.

Most of my waking life—some of it rewarding, some of it not—was not spent writing but working, earning a living: preparing classes, teaching classes, sitting in English department meetings.[1] Also laboring on those faculty committees that come with tenure, organizing graduate programs, supervising theses, and even taking up campus-related causes and getting involved in court scrapes . . . finding lawyers for students divorcing abusive husbands, writing to a judge for a student arrested for stealing bedsprings in an abandoned farmhouse, forming a defense committee for a Venezuelan colleague threatened by his government for exposing the drug trade in its tuna fleet—in other words, taking on causes one never thought to be involved in but that one felt could not be ignored, like the time my wife and I took in, at our remote farmhouse, Jane Fonda, Tom Hayden, and their five-person entourage from the Indochina Peace Campaign when the actress and activist came to talk at our university. But that's another story.

Then there's the writer's everyday work at home that every husband does: the garden and trees, fencing to keep in the pets, fixing this, painting that, and participating in the daily talk of who needs what and what should be done, etc., etc.

Not to mention the *business realm* of writing: sending off manuscripts and waiting for replies, sometimes for months, sometimes for never, with poetry increasingly hard to sell to its ever-dwindling audience. Oh, there are so many ways that writers can fritter away time from their writing. "Doing reviews," my former teacher John Barth once advised me as my own books started to appear, "isn't a good way to spend your time, and inevitably makes enemies." Oh, how to find time, how to extend time, *bend* it. Early on at Penn State, whining about trying to find time to write, I was handed a rather large bottle of amphetamine by a professor who said it had been left him by Barth a decade earlier. *Possibly.* I mean, I understood its line of inheritance but I doubted the provenance of this particular gift, given Barth's staunch propriety.

Some writing-related but time-wasting ventures can be both fun and incredibly promising, even if finally useless. Like trying to sell movie rights. (Make a pile! Retire to your writing!) My memoir about Vietnam, *Remembering Heaven's Face,* and a novel, *Coming Down Again,* attracted some movie interest. The novel, with characters based on my friends Steve Erhart, John Steinbeck, and Rosie Boycott, was set first in London, where Steve had cancer treatment, and then in India—on Steve's way back to Vietnam—where he died a few weeks later, accompanied by Steinbeck and Rosie, who, after cremating Steve and continuing on to Vietnam, managed to get themselves imprisoned by the Thai Border Patrol when they crossed the border from the Burmese Golden Triangle. It was a good story and it got me fancy dinners in Los Angeles with movie people and an option on the movie rights that I sold to a cinematographer. ("Mr. Balaban, I am sitting here in the Philippine jungle where I am shooting another shallow Vietnam movie and reading your novel on breaks. Would you be interested in selling movie rights?") I sold him a six-month option and visited him at his studio in Topanga Canyon as he tried to raise the funding for production. And at dinner I met Stephen Peck, Gregory Peck's son, who had been a lieutenant in the Marines in Vietnam and who was interested in the memoir, but my most hopeful prospects came from a pair of HBO producers who drove from New York to work with me on a script in my attic study in State College, Pennsylvania. Good guys, clever and funny, but unfortunately they soon were out of jobs in a corporate shuffle. So it was all, in the sense of this essay, wasted time. But fun, briefly.

To do any actual writing, I always had to get away from work and home. On school breaks, I tried friends' farms and beach houses and got some good work done. I even tried a small metal trailer on a pine-darkened mountainside in the Poconos, where I looked around and left after two hours in its damp gloom. There was also, albeit briefly, a sunny room over a restaurant in southern Spain in the mountains near Málaga.

My best places—where I got the most written—were writer havens like the Lannan Foundation in Marfa, Texas, and the Helene Wurlitzer Foundation in Taos, New Mexico. I had a six-month stay at the Wurlitzer while on academic leave, and I finished a novel as well as a book of poetry, *Locusts at the Edge of Summer*. At both places the management was helpfully available and never intruding. And while there were other writers in other houses, you didn't have to meet them if you didn't want to. Neither place had a common eating area or even an office where you could pick up your mail. So both places were *perfect*.

In Taos, I also made lifelong friends with folks in town and at the library. We named our daughter after one of the gallery owners, and thirty years later I still correspond with two of the guys who ran the Harwood Library on Ledoux Street down past Tally Richards's Gallery of Contemporary Art.

What is *outside* a writer's house can be as important as what's inside. The canyons and creeks around Taos became my most instructive places, talking to me as I talked to myself . . . while walking down the huge Rio Grande gorge cutting through the high plains or the cliffs and waterfall above Arroyo Seco or on a strip of land of nearby Tiwa property where one of the elders gave me the okay to walk.

— • —

In the late spring of 2016, I heard from friends in Santa Fe that a friend of theirs was looking for someone to look after the family ranch for a month or so, and in a place so remote it wasn't easily found on Google Maps. Right off, I said yes and soon got a letter—quoted in part below—from the daughter of the owner, who had built condominiums in New York and had recently died, leaving his widow to sell the place and bring his ashes back East.

Dear John,

I'm not sure what precisely Carola passed on about this opportunity, so I will be as precise as possible.

My father passed away this winter. He had been living for 15 years or so in a 2600' log cabin which he built on land he settled, about 2.5 miles off of 25N in Tecolote, NM. Tecolote is 10 miles south of Las Vegas, NM and if you have never been there, I have no doubt you could write several poems about it—as it is a place where things happen but are rarely, if ever, seen. Lots of strange history though.

The house sits on 40 acres of land. There is another dweller not far off, though one cannot see his home.

The views from the house are beautiful and unobstructed.

It is quiet and peaceful, sometimes hot, sometimes dusty.

The road from [I-]25 is long and sometimes bumpy, but rarely problematic, though AWD or a car that is not too low is helpful.

—J.H.

I-25 runs from southern New Mexico north to Wyoming. It's the old Santa Fe trail, the route the first conquistadors took as they steered out of the steep Sangre de Cristo, the southern Rockies, for the safety of the more open Llano Estacado, with its capstone cliffs and mesas extending into the endless, flat, wide-open, high desert dotted with piñon, juniper, mesquite, and cactus. Francisco Vázquez de Coronado, on his 1541 expedition to find the golden city of Cíbola, described the Llano Estacado running from eastern New Mexico up into Colorado and down into the Oklahoma handle and northern Texas:

I reached some plains so vast, that I did not find their limit anywhere I went, although I traveled over them for [nearly 800 miles] . . . with no more land marks than if we had been swallowed up by the sea . . . there was not a stone, nor bit of rising ground, nor a tree, nor a shrub, nor anything to go by.[2]

My ranch-sitting was in that high desert a few miles outside Tecolote, population 235, just off I-25. *Tecolote* means "owl" in Nahuatl, a Mexican Indian word suggesting the pre-Columbian origins of the trail. A creek trickles through Tecolote. In 1824, its sheep and farming settlement received a land grant from Mexico. By 1846, after our border war, it was part of the United States. For a while, Tecolote prospered as a stop on the Santa Fe Trail and as a military outpost fighting the Comanche and other tribes that had threatened the town since its beginning. It still has an active church, Nuestra Señora de Dolores, but no store, gas station, or post office. These all disappeared after Route 66 and a new railroad bypassed the town.

In July 2016 I was headed for the ranch off the Camino del Leon, a windy dirt road that scraped the bottom of the little car I had rented at the Albuquerque airport as I bumped along, passing a few property fences overhung by junipers until the road just seemed to end in a sparse forest of puny little trees, dusty foot trails, and washouts. But there I was, looking through a rail gate to a red-roofed, log-sided house way up at the end of a long graveled lane.

On my first morning, I made some coffee and set up my computer and printer. Buckets of sunlight poured through the windows. I walked outside, where pine trees dotted the property, scenting the morning air. Farther off from the shaded front porch, I found an electrical shack, a tool-shed, and the carport under a slant of rough-cut viga rafters, but there was nothing else in sight except, to my surprise as I continued on, a swimming pool filled with algae and, beyond that, an old attempt at a pond that was now mostly dried up.

I figured I ought to take a little walk before breakfast and get the lay of the land, so I headed up the gravel lane to the road and squeezed through the gate where the Camino seemed to end in a scatter of little tracks and paths disappearing into the junipers and piñon.

This was a mistake. July in New Mexico and I didn't have a hat. But it was a cool morning. Then again, I was only thinking maybe a twenty-minute walk straight in, turn around, and just follow my footprints back to the ranch. Anyway, I had a cell phone, albeit a not-too-smart flip top, so I figured I could call for help in the unlikelihood of a snakebite, or scorpion sting, or whatever. Keeping the sun at my back as a directional marker and taking what looked like a jeep path through the diminutive pines and being careful not to jam my sneaker toes into prickly pear cactus, I walked until I found an old dammed-up pond shaded by some sizable ponderosa pines. I wondered who kept livestock here.

My twenty minutes had expired and I couldn't have gone a mile before deciding to go a little farther to see what I could see because so far it wasn't that interesting. The landscape wasn't, as Coronado noted, without tree, or shrub, or rising ground; it was *nothing but* scrubby little trees, cholla cactus, rocks, and boulders, with spiny ocotillo scattered all about parched hills and their networks of dusty trails—man-made? How old? Were there deer out there? There was even the kind of cactus called "jumping cholla." The tops of the trees were over my head, so my field of vision couldn't find the horizon or make out any real landmarks in the beyond. I was getting thirsty in the dry heat. Prudence told me to turn around. I looked down to find my footprints and started back.

An hour or so later, I lost my footprints altogether in the twisting trails through the junipers—and it was hot, really hot, with the sun on my scalp. The network of paths led this way and that. I listened for the sound of cars or trucks to indicate I-25 and its north–south direction but heard nothing except a vague susurrus of crickets, grasshoppers, and other insects—no bird calls, no distant voices, no cars or trucks, or even faint highway drone.

Hours later, I was completely lost and getting dizzy from stumbling over the rocky terrain in the heat. I was seventy-two years old that summer and had just had a heart implant the year before. (I know. I know. What was I even doing out there alone?) I just kept walking. Once, in Vietnam, during the siege of a city that was partly overrun and about to fall, I took refuge at a nearby air force base. When it looked like the base would also fall, I considered how I was going to say goodbye to my family back home. If I were shot dead, my watch and wallet would get picked by the NVA or Viet Cong. So I wrote a note and stuffed it in my jeans' back pocket over my butt where, I reasoned, even if I were shot, the note might survive bloodied but readable. Now, on this first day of my current adventure in the Writing Life, swallowing my pride, I figured it might be time to make my cell phone call to my wife, tell her what was happening, and ask her to call the state police in nearby Las Vegas, New Mexico.

Of course, there was no cell phone signal.

And, as I was sitting there on a little cathedral of crumbly rock and staring at the flip top, a huge snake—I mean really big, fat and four feet long, with black and yellow markings—pulled away from underneath the rocks and slithered off into the brush. Since I couldn't just sit there (because no one was going to find me until the vultures started circling), I got up, picked another dubious path, and plodded on.

I finally found myself on a hillcrest that let me see farther than ten feet. Now, looking around in all directions across the miles of treetops glinting in the sunshine, I saw a tin roof way off in the distance and started toward it. But distances are deceiving in clear dry air.

Soon it was noon, and I was still walking toward that bright tin roof, hoping to find the building and some water. Eventually I climbed another and steeper hilltop and saw the rooftop and its small farmhouse fenced by barbed wire, so I skidded down the hillside toward it.

I called into the house from across the barbed wire but got no answer. Then I crawled through, worried that I might get shot. But the place was empty. Out in the yard, near an empty chicken coop, I found a hand pump, but it was dry. I considered walking down the dirt road leading to the house, but clearly nothing had been down that weed-choked rut in a long time.

Farther off in the distance was a railroad track. I figured it had to go somewhere, one way or the other, and I made my way to it, slipping as I climbed up its gravel embankment, until I found myself standing, wobbly and sunburned and thirsty, but free in the open and thankfully clear of the scrub forest. But which of the two ways to go? Exhausted, I started off down the miles of gravel bed, spaced wooden ties, and iron rails.

After some miles, I heard a *beep-beep* behind me. I thought I was hallucinating. You know . . . *beep-beep*—like in a Road Runner cartoon? My thinking flushed, addled and indignant, I turned around to a *truck* on the rails right behind me. Instead of truck tires, it had rail rims. It was a train-repair truck, and its driver was waving me over.

"What the hell are you doing out here?!" he shouted as he opened his passenger door and shoved aside some water bottles to make room for me on the seat.

It was air-conditioned.

I couldn't talk but took the water bottle that he opened and handed me, and then I explained that I was staying at a house somewhere nearby and somehow got lost.

"Look," he said, "I have work to do up ahead and I can't take you anywhere except the next road. Do you want me to call the state police?" He pointed to his CB radio.

I emptied the bottle. "How long would that take?"

"Out here? Maybe hours."

"I think you saved my life," I said.

He was a repairman for BNSF, the Burlington Northern Santa Fe. The last thing I wanted was to get out of his truck to wait for the cops to take me to a hospital as I am sure they would be required to do. I felt so stupid.

So I rode with him in his air-conditioned railcar, drinking his water, until we reached a dirt road crossing where he did something really clever and kind: he stopped his truck on the railroad blocking the road to any traffic and waited with me until a pickup truck came along. Then, telling me to stay put and cool off, he got out and walked over to the pickup and talked its driver into taking me out to I-25, where the driver—as it turned out, an old Vietnam vet living by himself out in the hills—dropped me at the on-ramp where, once more, I was baking in the heat. After a while I hitched a second ride that took me to the Tecolote turnoff. From there, I walked the two to three miles back up the Camino del Leon, squeezed through the metal gate onto the gravel driveway, and collapsed inside my shady ranch house. I had been lost for about five hours and—looking at a map the next day—had walked about fifteen miles all told.

I never got the repairman's name. I think he said Archuleta, and I think of him every time I watch the PBS evening news with its BNSF advertisement.

Oh, the writing life.

1. Andrew Delbanco memorably mentions English departments in his "The Decline and Fall of Literature," *The New York Review of Books,* Nov. 4, 1999, quoting Carol Christ, provost at UC Berkeley: "On every campus there is one department whose name need only be mentioned to make people laugh; you don't want that department to be yours."
2. See the Texas State Historical Association for more: https://www.tshaonline.org/texas -day-by-day/entry/113.

Acknowledgments

These poems, essays, and translations have been previously published by Copper Canyon Press in *Empires* (2019); *Path, Crooked Path* (2006); *Locusts at the Edge of Summer: New & Selected Poems* (1997, 2003); *Words for My Daughter* (1991); *Ca Dao Việt Nam: Vietnamese Folk Poetry* (2003); and *Spring Essence: The Poetry of Hồ Xuân Hương* (2000).

Versions of the poems have also appeared in the following journals: *Alaska Quarterly Review; American Poet: The Journal of the Academy of American Poets; The American Scholar; Approach; The Atlantic; Blackbox Manifold; Chasing Out the Demons; Chelsea; Cimarron Review; Colorado Review; Connecticut Review; Electrum; Friends Journal; Fugue; Gargoyle; Granta; Great River Review; Green Mountains Review; Harper's; The Hudson Review; I-70 Review; The Journal of American Culture; Leviathan Quarterly; Literary Matters; The Massachusetts Review; The McNeese Review; Michigan Quarterly Review; The Nation; Neon; New England Review; New Letters; New Mexico Poetry Review; The New York Review of Books; The New York Times; Nhạc Thơ Hân Thương; Painted Bride Quarterly; Perfect Dragonfly; Ploughshares; Poet Lore; Poetry; Poetry Flash; Poetry Now; Prairie Schooner; Rattle; The Ruminator Review; The Sewanee Review; Solo; Southern Humanities Review; The Southern Review; Spillway; Tar River Poetry; TriQuarterly; Valparaiso Poetry Review; Verse; Virginia Quarterly Review; Walter Magazine; War, Literature & the Arts; Western Humanities Review;* and *Witness.*

About the Author

JOHN BALABAN is the author of fourteen books of poetry and prose, including four volumes that together have won the Academy of American Poets' James Laughlin Award, a National Poetry Series Selection, and two nominations for the National Book Award. His book *Locusts at the Edge of Summer: New & Selected Poems* won the 1998 William Carlos Williams Award from the Poetry Society of America. In 2003, he was awarded a Guggenheim Fellowship, and in 2005, he was a judge for the National Book Awards. Balaban served as a conscientious objector during the war in Vietnam. In addition to writing poetry, fiction, and nonfiction, he is a translator of Vietnamese poetry and a past president of the American Literary Translators Association. In 1999, with two Vietnamese friends, he founded the Vietnamese Nôm Preservation Foundation (nomfoundation.org). In 2008, he was awarded a medal from Vietnam's Ministry of Culture for his poetry translations and his leadership in the restoration of the ancient text collection at the National Library. www.johnbalaban.com.

Poetry is vital to language and living. Since 1972, Copper Canyon Press has published extraordinary poetry from around the world to engage the imaginations and intellects of readers, writers, booksellers, librarians, teachers, students, and donors.

WE ARE GRATEFUL FOR THE MAJOR SUPPORT PROVIDED BY:

academy of american poets

CULTURE

Hawthornden Foundation

INGRAM CONTENT GROUP

Lannan

 ART WORKS. | National Endowment for the Arts arts.gov

OFFICE OF ARTS & CULTURE
SEATTLE

THE PAUL G. ALLEN FAMILY FOUNDATION

POETRY FOUNDATION

the point envision·enact·evolve

WASHINGTON STATE ARTS COMMISSION

The Witter Bynner Foundation for Poetry

TO LEARN MORE ABOUT UNDERWRITING
COPPER CANYON PRESS TITLES,
PLEASE CALL 360-385-4925 EXT. 103

WE ARE GRATEFUL FOR THE MAJOR SUPPORT PROVIDED BY:

Anonymous

Richard Andrews and
    Colleen Chartier

Jill Baker and Jeffrey Bishop

Anne and Geoffrey Barker

Donna Bellew

Will Blythe

John Branch

Diana Broze

John R. Cahill

Sarah Cavanaugh

Keith Cowan and Linda Walsh

Peter Currie

Stephanie Ellis-Smith and
    Douglas Smith

Mimi Gardner Gates

Gull Industries Inc.
    on behalf of William True

Carolyn and Robert Hedin

David and Jane Hibbard

Bruce S. Kahn

Phil Kovacevich and Eric Wechsler

Maureen Lee and Mark Busto

Ellie Mathews and Carl Youngmann
    as The North Press

Larry Mawby and Lois Bahle

Petunia Charitable Fund and
    adviser Elizabeth Hebert

Suzanne Rapp and Mark Hamilton

Adam and Lynn Rauch

Emily and Dan Raymond

Joseph C. Roberts

Cynthia Sears

Kim and Jeff Seely

Tree Swenson

Barbara and Charles Wright

In honor of C.D. Wright,
    from Forrest Gander

Caleb Young as C. Young Creative

The dedicated interns and faithful
    volunteers of Copper Canyon Press

The pressmark for Copper Canyon Press
suggests entrance, connection, and interaction
while holding at its center
an attentive, dynamic space for poetry.

This book is set in EB Garamond.
Book design by Gopa & Ted2, Inc.
Printed on archival-quality paper.